Helen's

Mix & Match

QUILTING PATTERNS

Helen Squire

American Quilter's Society

Dear Helen Series • *Book Seven*

Located in Paducah, Kentucky, the American Quilter's Society (AQS) is dedicated to promoting the accomplishments of today's quilters. Through its publications and events, AQS strives to honor today's quiltmakers and their work and to inspire future creativity and innovation in quiltmaking.

EDITOR: HELEN SQUIRE
GRAPHIC DESIGN & ILLUSTRATIONS: LYNDA SMITH
COVER DESIGN & ILLUSTRATIONS: MICHAEL BUCKINGHAM
PHOTOGRAPHY: CHARLES R. LYNCH, UNLESS OTHERWISE NOTED

Library of Congress Cataloging-in-Publication Data
Squire, Helen.
  Helen's mix & match quilting patterns / by Helen Squire.
    p. cm.
  Summary: "Features over 100 patterns that can be adapted from hand to machine quilting and vice versa. Includes placement diagrams, combinations, helpful hints and a range of designs"--Provided by publisher.
    ISBN 1-57432-887-5
    1. Quilting--Patterns. I. Title: Helen's mix and match quilting patterns. II. Title: Mix & match quilting patterns. III. Title.

  TT835.S6673 2005
  746.46'041--dc22

                          2005015947

Additional copies of this book may be ordered from the American Quilter's Society, PO Box 3290, Paducah, KY 42002-3290; Toll Free: 800-626-5420, or online at www.AmericanQuilter.com.

Copyright © 2005, Helen Squire

Dedication

To Janie Donaldson, Sally Terry, Cheryl Barnes, and Judy Allen. Thank you for your friendship, and the pleasure and privilege of being your AQS book editor. I admire your considerable talents.

To Karen McTavish. In appreciation for graciously quilting the book's cover pattern. I love the combination of my design with your "McTavishing" technique.

And as always, to my daughters, Laura, Susan, and Vanessa.

Contents

Contents

Introduction

I am in the enviable position of having edited *Add-a-Line Continuous Quilting Patterns* and *Add-a-Line Continued*, both by Janie Donaldson; *Pathways to Better Quilting* by Sally Terry; *The Best of Shirley Thompson Quilting Patterns* by Cheryl Barnes; *The Art of Feather Quilting* by Judy Allen; and I am currently editing *Beautiful Quilts as You Go* by Keryn Emmerson. This is a powerful line-up of quilting expertise, their artistic talents and professional know-how all geared to today's quilters. I am both honored and proud to be involved in the publication of their American Quilter's Society books.

So, you might think it's funny how a traditional hand quilter like myself became immersed in machine quilting – but the common denominator is the design process. The quilting patterns in the entire Dear Helen collection (this is the seventh in the series) can easily be adapted from hand to machine quilting, and vice versa. These patterns are ready to trace, scan, or photocopy. You have my written permission to do so, but not to resell the patterns.

I will show how to mix and match patterns and have included helpful hints along with secondary design ideas and borders with companion blocks wherever possible. Over 100 patterns have been grouped into these categories/chapters: More Helen's Hints, Framing Ideas, Traditional Patterns, Continuous Line, Beautiful Scrolls, Grids VII, and Secondary Designs.

With over 30 years of teaching experience, the question most frequently asked me is still the same – How do you mark the quilting design onto the quilt? Even though I believe it's not *how* you mark, it's *what* you mark that is important, I have included more details and illustrated examples of what I do use. See Utilizing Plastic Stencils with Preplanning on page 33, making a Muslin Master Pattern on page 59, and Grids VII on page 90.

Three of my larger format books are out of print. I have included some of those original quilting patterns, redrawn and re-purposed, rather than have them lost and forgotten. Most are still available as stencils by Quilting Creations International. There are now 650 quilting patterns in the Dear Helen Series and that's not counting the countless different size variations that are on my CD-ROMS, *Helen's Print & Use Quilting Patterns* and *Create & Print with Helen Squire*. I hope you use them all!

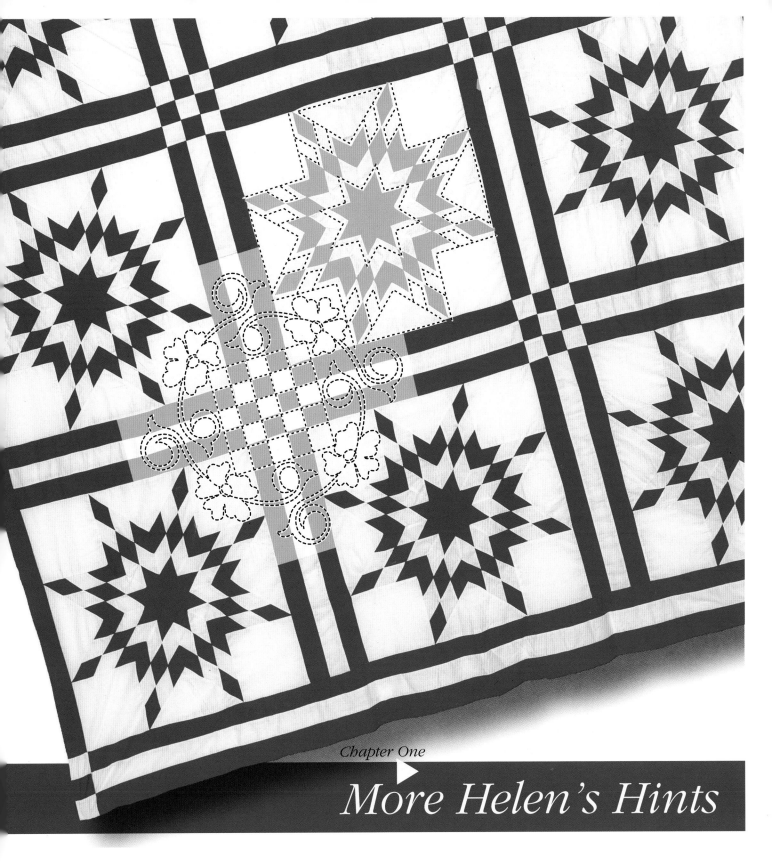

Chapter One

▶ More Helen's Hints

It's very common to read "quilt as desired." There are many good books and articles on piecing with excellent sewing advice, but reference sources are scarce when it comes to deciding "what and where" to begin quilting.

A good design rule is: When the pattern (quilt top) is geometric the quilting should be flowing. The eye is sat-

isfied and the arrangement is more pleasing with straight lines and curved quilting.

The solid red and white star quilt, shown above, with its multiple blocks, strong linear sashing strips, and checkerboard intersection, is the perfect place to begin planning a fancy quilting design!

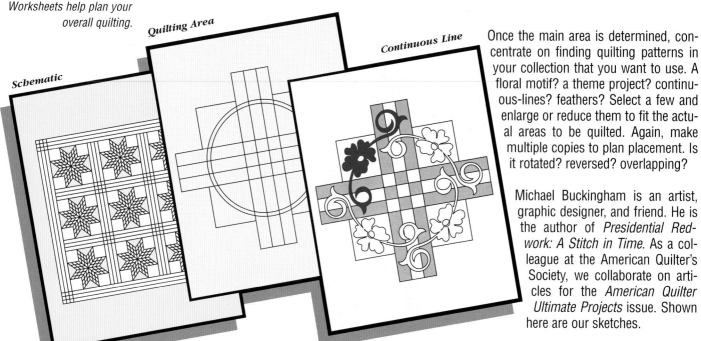

Worksheets help plan your overall quilting.

Schematic

Quilting Area

Continuous Line

Once the main area is determined, concentrate on finding quilting patterns in your collection that you want to use. A floral motif? a theme project? continuous-lines? feathers? Select a few and enlarge or reduce them to fit the actual areas to be quilted. Again, make multiple copies to plan placement. Is it rotated? reversed? overlapping?

Michael Buckingham is an artist, graphic designer, and friend. He is the author of *Presidential Redwork: A Stitch in Time.* As a colleague at the American Quilter's Society, we collaborate on articles for the *American Quilter Ultimate Projects* issue. Shown here are our sketches.

The quilting possibilities are endless once you identify and establish *the area to be quilted.* This is best done with a worksheet or schematic of the actual seam lines. I used a 50% reduction for my drawings. It's fun to start thinking outside the box, identifying areas where secondary designs will add drama. Usually we quilt a pattern within the perimeter of each block, then use another in the sashing. Look again at the quilt top photograph and see how focusing the quilting design around the intersection of the blocks and sashing, a secondary design, makes a stronger statement.

Whether you are planning to quilt by hand or by machine will influence your final quilting pattern, but what I want to share with you is how to determine where to quilt. Structural quilting is based on the type of batting you have selected. Obviously, cotton batting requires closer quilting lines while a thick polyester batt allows for larger unquilted spaces.

For this star quilt, I determined that the checkerboard intersections and triple-wide sashing strips were going to be the main quilting area. The stars themselves would be quilted-in-the-ditch around the shape and the predominate color placement of the diamonds. The 6" white corner squares would be treated as "whipped cream" areas (no seam allowances underneath), showcasing the major portions of the quilting pattern. The nine-patch is transformed into a 25-patch by extending the 2" gridlines.

Make multiple copies of your worksheet (at least five copies) or better yet, tape transparent paper on top of your colored-in sketch. After you draw in minimal quilting lines (normally the quilt-in-the-ditch sections) simply lift the page away from the sketch and *see* what the back of the quilt will look like, *determine* if enough quilting has been planned, and *decide* if you like the overall design you have chosen.

Once the placement and final design is chosen, it is time to redraw it accurately and make a marking device. Quilt tops are best marked before batting-up. For this red and white quilt it's easy to trace the pattern on the top using a light source underneath. Another idea is to fold rolls of transparent paper to make layered copies, needle punch along the design lines, then position and pin as needed on the quilt top – a No-Marking Method developed by Golden Threads.

I recommend using a color-matched chalk pencil or pounce to mark the lines. Mark lightly. You can always refer to the quilting design pattern and worksheet to see "what and where" you planned to quilt.

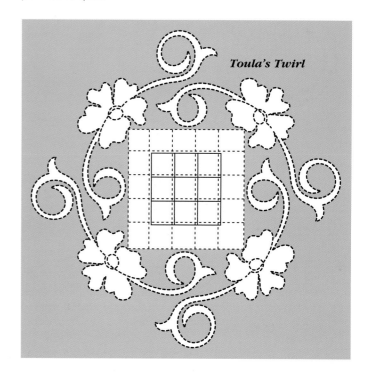

Toula's Twirl

- ❏ To prevent the design from "floating" in an area too big for its size, use a circle to frame the quilting pattern. It will lock in the background fullness and showcase the main motif.

- ❏ The full-sized pattern for *Toula's Twirl* is provided on page 69. It can be enlarged to any size.

- ❏ Also on that page is the secondary design formed when the design is placed edge-to-edge and used as a pantograph pattern.

Toula's Twirl
7"

Quilting UFOs

Lately I have been teaching classes on *How-to Quilt those UFOs* (Unfinished Objects). The two questions I ask are What method of quilting are you using? and What type of batting are you planning to use? It is important to know if it's by hand or machine, and if it's a low or high loft batt *before* you decide on the overall quilting pattern(s).

I own this antique quilt top, so I can be critical as well as offer helpful advice. The close-up photograph on the next page — one-quarter of the pieced block — shows pitfalls to avoid in quilting. My overall design solution is *Mary's Meandering Leaves Variation*, shown above. Turn to page 67 for the full-sized pattern and more advice.

Here is an example of the type of suggestions I also offer –

Quilting in-the-ditch (along the side without extra seam allowances underneath) around the squares ❶ in this *Mother's Choice* block locks in the fullness and stabilizes the area to be quilted. The red stars ❷ begin to shine and stand out from the background when the entire star shape is raised by the in-the-ditch quilting.

Do *not* quilt the individual seams ❸ along the entire large block. They are all different sizes and that method of quilting would only emphasize that irregularity. Consider using a *Double Wedding Ring* or *Robbing Peter to Pay Paul* shape to connect the blocks.

When the same colored fabric is pieced together, it should be considered as an entire design unit and quilted as a whole. Do *not* quilt each diamond or triangle separately. While structurally correct, it is not the best choice for this block. Outline quilting ❹ that connects the overall shapes used in the *Mother's Choice* block will work better (i.e., the red star, the gold framework).

Inside the eight pointed star, you have three choices: ⑤ⓐ outline quilt ¼" *away* from each seam; ⑤ⓑ use a softer curved quilting line similar to that used in Hawaiian appliqué quilts, or ⑤ⓒ outline quilt ½" *inside* the seams creating a smaller star shape.

Select any free-motion quilting design ❻ to connect the gold triangles forming the outer, circular look of the block. Use a small-to-medium-size scale. This type of quilting motif is better because it crosses over the bulk from the underneath seams, and it will camouflage the unequal points in the finished quilt top. If you used outline quilting or quilting in-the-ditch on the gold pieces, it would only emphases the piecing irregularities.

PITFALLS TO AVOID IN QUILTING

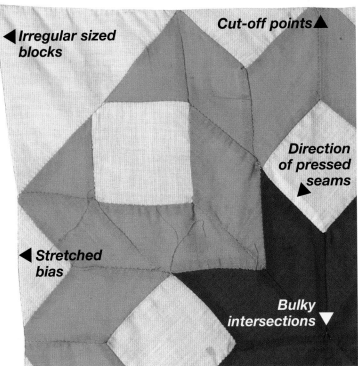

◀ *Irregular sized blocks*

Cut-off points ▲

Direction of pressed seams ▼

◀ *Stretched bias*

Bulky intersections ▼

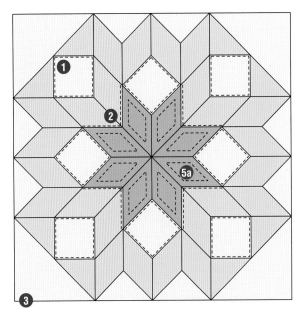

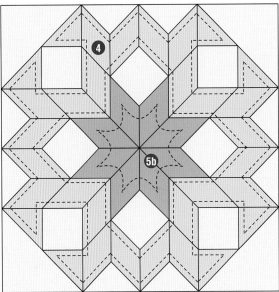

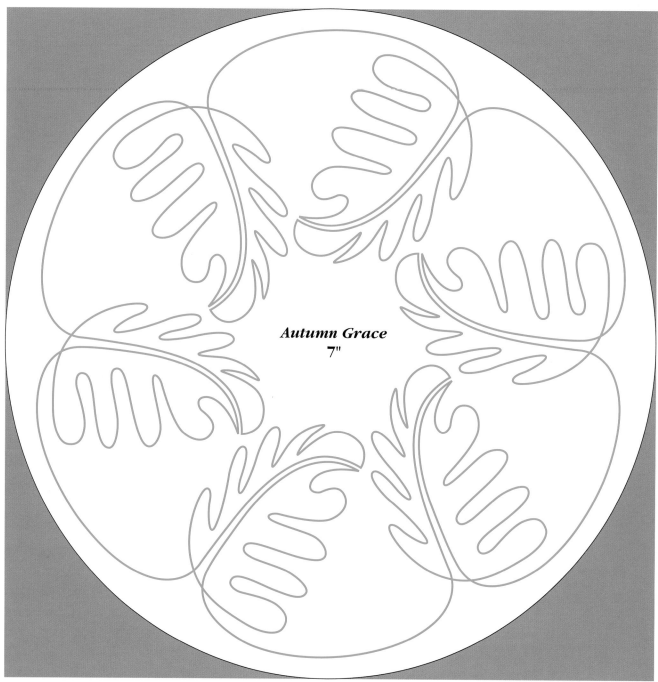

Autumn Grace
7"

Placement Diagram – The leaves of *Autumn Grace* face inward and clockwise, surrounded by a circle.

☐ The Amazing Grace Border & Block series (pages 12–15) originated at a quilt show where I experimented on The Grace Machine Quilter, a hand-guided frame used with a domestic sewing machine. I stitched the pattern free-hand and then copied the design onto paper.

☐ It's easy to plan mix & match patterns using the same basic design. These can be traced, photocopied, or scanned.

☐ You have my written permission to copy the patterns in this book for personal use and to professionally quilt.

☐ Making a reversed tracing is very important. Left and right versions are needed to miter a corner. Also when you quilt left-handed or on a sewing machine, it becomes easier when the design faces clockwise.

☐ Longarm quilters might want the choice of reversing pantograph rows. A reverse pattern helps.

☐ Notice that some quilting patterns have a dot and an arrow to signify continuous lines. They are not meant to be starting and stopping points, only suggestions.

Graceful Leaf
7" Continuous

Pattern can be reversed, enlarged, or reduced to any size.

Placement Diagram – Leaves are placed for edge-to-edge quilting in *Graceful Leaves*.

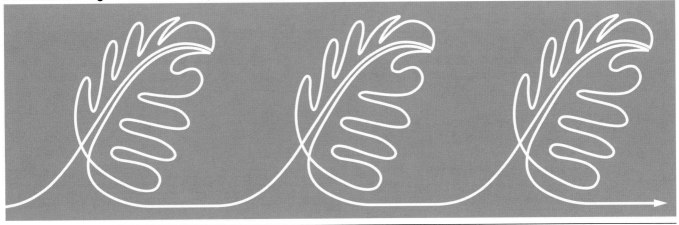

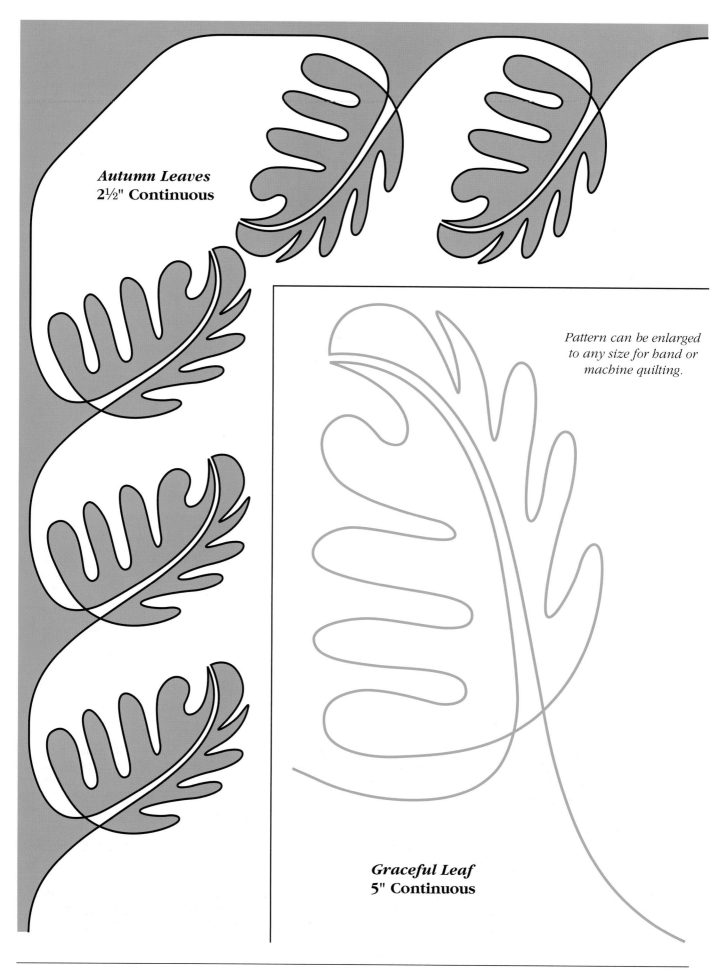

Autumn Leaves
2½" Continuous

*Pattern can be enlarged
to any size for hand or
machine quilting.*

Graceful Leaf
5" Continuous

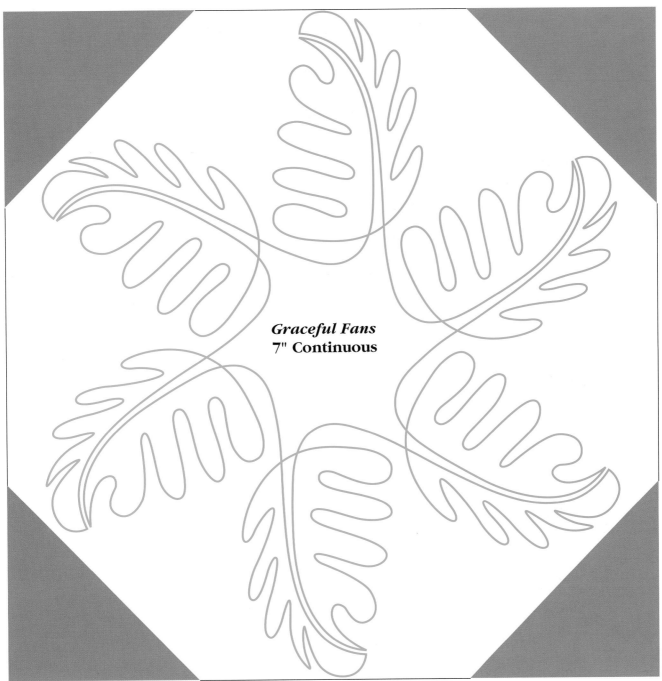

Graceful Fans
7" Continuous

Placement Diagram – Leaves of *Graceful Fans* face outward and counter-clockwise inside of an octagon.

☐ The variety of variations with the Amazing Grace Border & Block series is awesome but the choices for pattern placement always remains the same. They are a proven formula for successful quilting.

☐ To make a companion block use multiple copies inside of any given area. Try a *circle*, *square*, *rectangle*, or *octagon* – whatever shape you need to fit your quilt.

☐ Face the patterns *inwards*, then try *outwards*. Look through the book for other examples of this simple technique (pages 42, 75, and 104).

☐ Use *left* facing patterns, then use the same layout with them facing *right*. Choose the pattern layout you like the best. Consider whether quilting by hand or machine.

☐ Minimize the background area by having some part of the pattern touch the surrounding shape. This locks in the fullness and prevents puffy areas that overwhelm the main motif.

☐ Make a good, clean copy for *marking* the quilting design. See Utilizing Plastic Stencils with Preplanning, page 33, and Muslin Master Pattern, page 59, for more information.

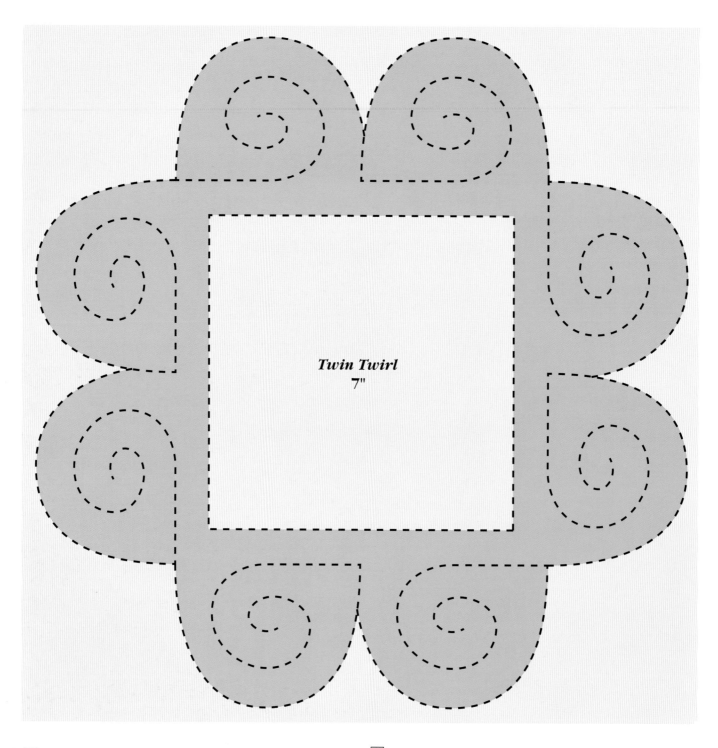

Twin Twirl
7"

As soon as they're finished, I always name my quilting patterns after family members and friends. This pair is christened after a duo of twirling six-year-olds, my twin grand-nephews, who have an abundance of energy and never seem to stop moving – just like the patterns.

The design screams for embellishments – machine quilting using exuberant thread hues, fancy embroidery stitches, or perhaps hand couching with bright, thick threads around the shape.

Both placement diagrams on page 17 illustrate two variations. ❶ and ❷ provide two different mitered corners. Ⓐ and Ⓑ show two versions of the pattern reversed at the center of the border.

Pay careful attention to the direction of the swirls when you mark your quilt using the large *Double Repeat* pattern on page 19. With extra copies, it can be made to rotate around the edges as well as be reversed and mirrored in your blocks and borders.

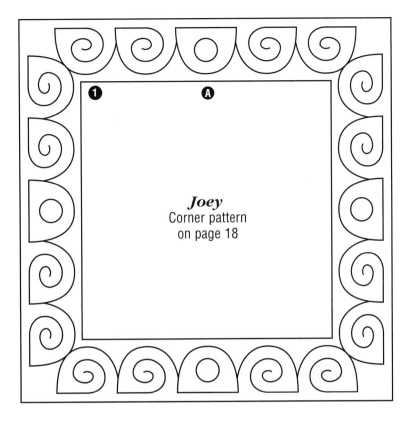

Joey
Corner pattern
on page 18

Placement Diagrams

Kevin
Corner pattern
on page 19

1" Toner Sashing Left

1" Toner Sashing Right

Joey's
Corner
2"

Placement Diagram

☐ The *Toner Sashing* pattern (page 17) was enlarged, copied with extra repeats, and extended. Then it was placed and rotated counter-clockwise around the edges of the quilt area.

Twin Twirl
2½" Double Repeat

Scan or trace, and reverse the pattern. It can then be enlarged or reduced to any size.

Kevin's Corner 2"

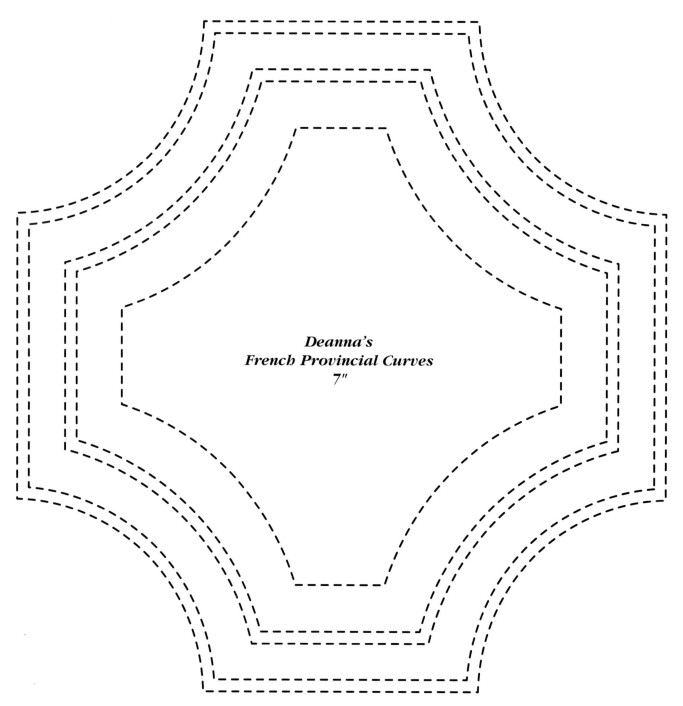

Deanna's
French Provincial Curves
7"

Chapter Two

▶ *Framing Ideas*

☐ Framing is an important new aspect to quilt design. Because of the ease and acceptance of mechanical quilting that adds stippling, meandering lines, curves, and shapes – any free-formed pattern – we want to flatten the background and establish the foreground of the design.

☐ This makes it necessary to clearly identify the area(s) of quilting, i.e., fluffy (less quilting) verses flat (more quilting), before we begin quilting. *Framing* the area helps.

☐ *The Barnes Collection* (pages 22–25) contains a framing worksheet with suggested shapes and sizes that frame the main quilting motif. See how *touching* the patterns can prevent the designs from *floating* in space.

☐ *The Tapestry Collection* (pages 28–31) has mixable patterns where the framing lines unify the patterns with built-in sashing strips.

☐ Multiple repeated blocks create secondary designs. See *More Moroccan* (page 26), *Bridger* (page 27), and *Woodbury* (page 32). They can be quilted by hand or machine.

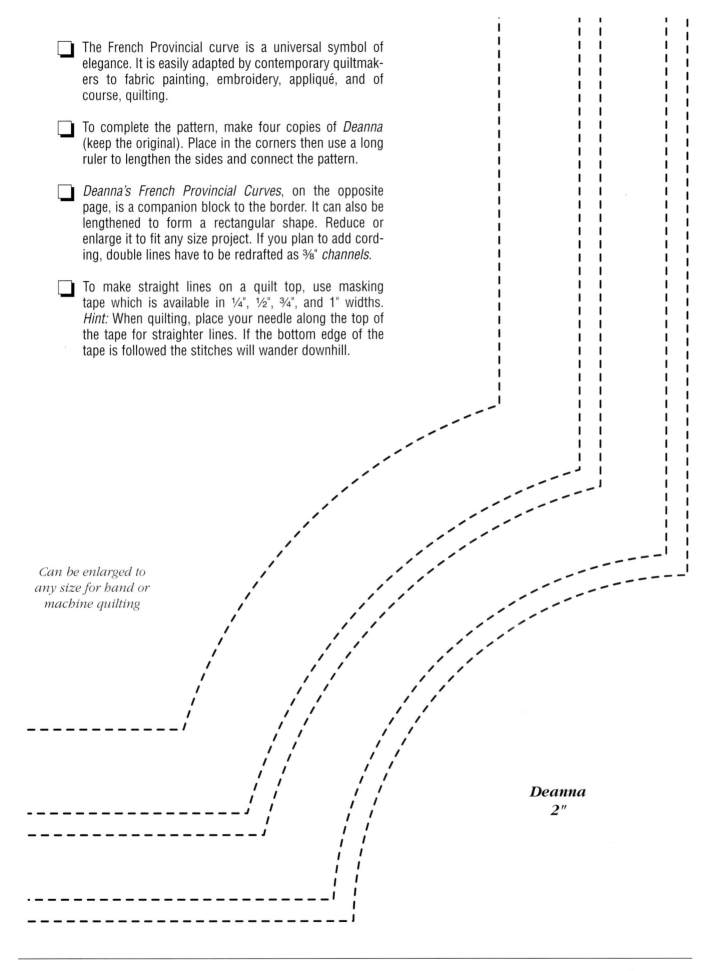

- The French Provincial curve is a universal symbol of elegance. It is easily adapted by contemporary quiltmakers to fabric painting, embroidery, appliqué, and of course, quilting.

- To complete the pattern, make four copies of *Deanna* (keep the original). Place in the corners then use a long ruler to lengthen the sides and connect the pattern.

- *Deanna's French Provincial Curves*, on the opposite page, is a companion block to the border. It can also be lengthened to form a rectangular shape. Reduce or enlarge it to fit any size project. If you plan to add cording, double lines have to be redrafted as ⅜" *channels*.

- To make straight lines on a quilt top, use masking tape which is available in ¼", ½", ¾", and 1" widths. *Hint:* When quilting, place your needle along the top of the tape for straighter lines. If the bottom edge of the tape is followed the stitches will wander downhill.

Can be enlarged to any size for hand or machine quilting

*Deanna
2"*

The Barnes Collection

Cheryl
6" x 6½"

The straight lines – representing sashings – complement the circular movement of the flowers and leaves, while effectively minimizing (reducing) the background area.

Reverse the design at the center of the pattern. Stretch or elongate as needed to fit any size area. Multiple repeats are then placed just touching, as shown below.

Secondary Design – The look of *Cheryl's Bouquet* can be enhanced with digital embroidery or thread painting.

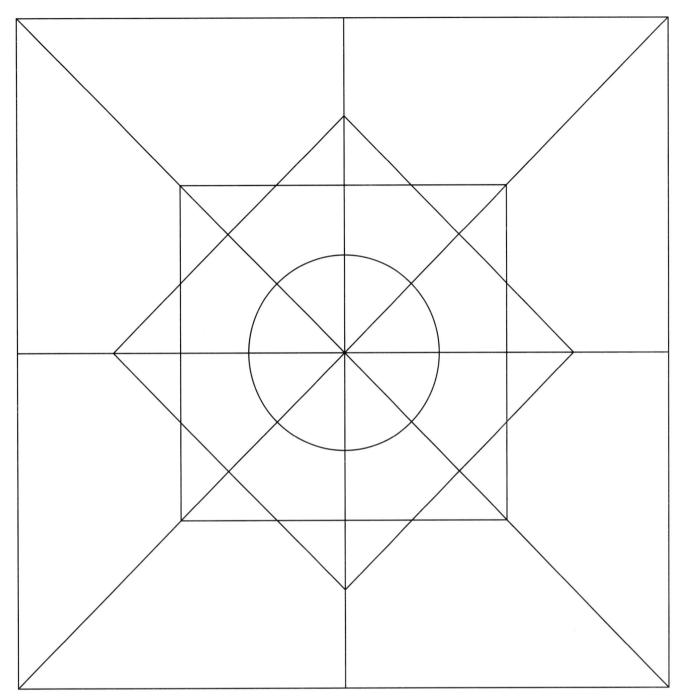

Placement Worksheet 7"

Imagine having a pretty little motif that you want to use in a quilt – perhaps an apple for a schoolhouse, or a cat or dog, or flowers. Anything too small to stand alone and command attention needs to be *framed*.

The Barnes Collection worksheet showcases shapes by dividing the background into smaller, geometric pieces. It is perfect for creating blocks that mix theme designs – whether they use appliqué, fusible, embroidered, or regular quilting patterns.

Illustrated above are some recommended divisions. The actual measurements depend on the size of your project. Shown on the worksheet above are a square frame, diagonal lines, quarter segments, a smaller box set square and on-point, and a center circle.

The fun part is combining these elements with the design motif. Consider using the worksheet as a *guideline* for placing the important motif. Refer to the four patterns on the following pages (pages 24–25) for some examples.

Silhouette Stencils

- Unify smaller motifs by combining them within a given area. Circular designs look better when joined with straight lines.

- The four blocks in the *Barnes Collection* have background areas divided into segments using *geometric shapes* – diagonal lines, diamonds, squares, and circles.

- Draw a 7" square block and use the main motif as a *silhouette stencil* (shown shaded) to *mark* the quilting pattern.

- First, trace the designs onto cardboard or manila folders and smoothly cut out their shapes.

- Next, use a ruler and compass (plastic circle combos work also) to divide the block. Position the motif as shown and mark around the silhouette stencil in a *continuous line* with a chalk colored pencil or a pretested water-erasable pen.

- This *marking technique* works well when the quilt top has already been batted-up or placed in a quilting frame.

Jason's Trail

Jim

**Silhouette
Stencil**

Cactus Jim

Benjamin's Ball

James

Ben

James'
Kaleidoscope

Jason

Silhouette
Stencils

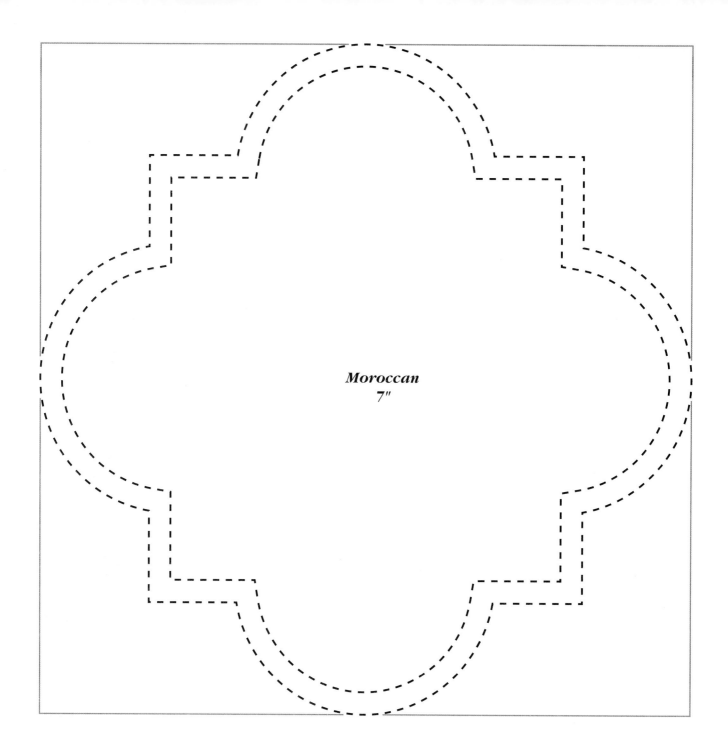

Moroccan
7"

Continuous Secondary Design

More Moroccan

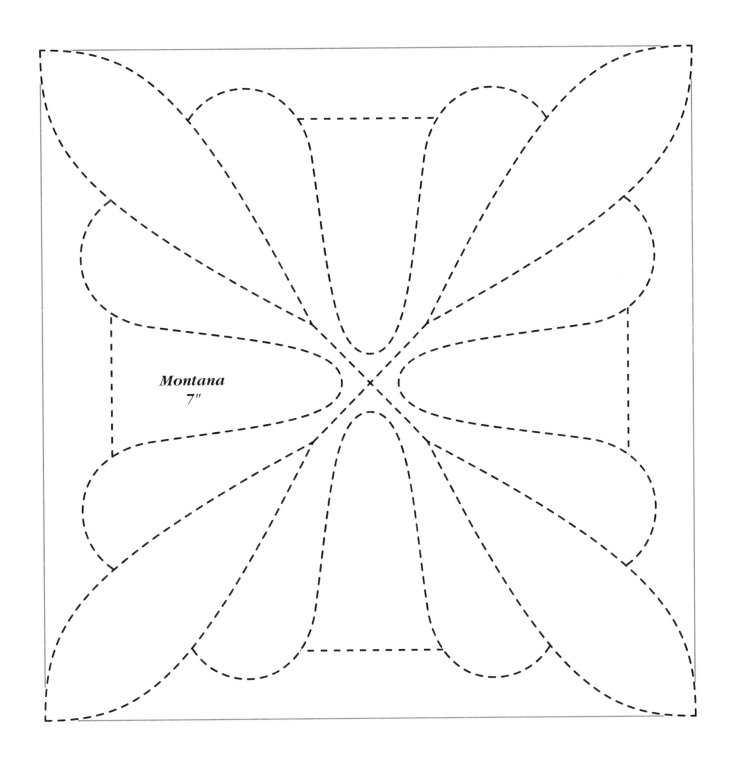

Montana
7"

Continuous Secondary Design

Bridger

Placement Diagram – The patterns in the *Tapestry Collection* create the illusion of a 2½" sashing strip (shown shaded).

❏ An elegant medieval tapestry once caught my eye and I rapidly sketched some placement possibilities. The *Tapestry Collection* is the result of my system of trial and error to develop patterns that really work – designs that can be quilted, as well as, appliquéd, embroidered, or even fused!

❏ Any beautiful design can then be enhanced with *framing*. Straight box-like lines showcase the floral shapes while *minimizing* the background area behind the design.

❏ In the placement diagram above, the three different patterns, *Abigail*, *Bethany*, and *Clarissa*, have been positioned on a diagonal setting with their tips just touching.

❏ As an added bonus, the straight lines look like sashing strips between the patterns. More quilting, perhaps using a crosshatch grid, would be required for structural support. It would depend on the type of batt used.

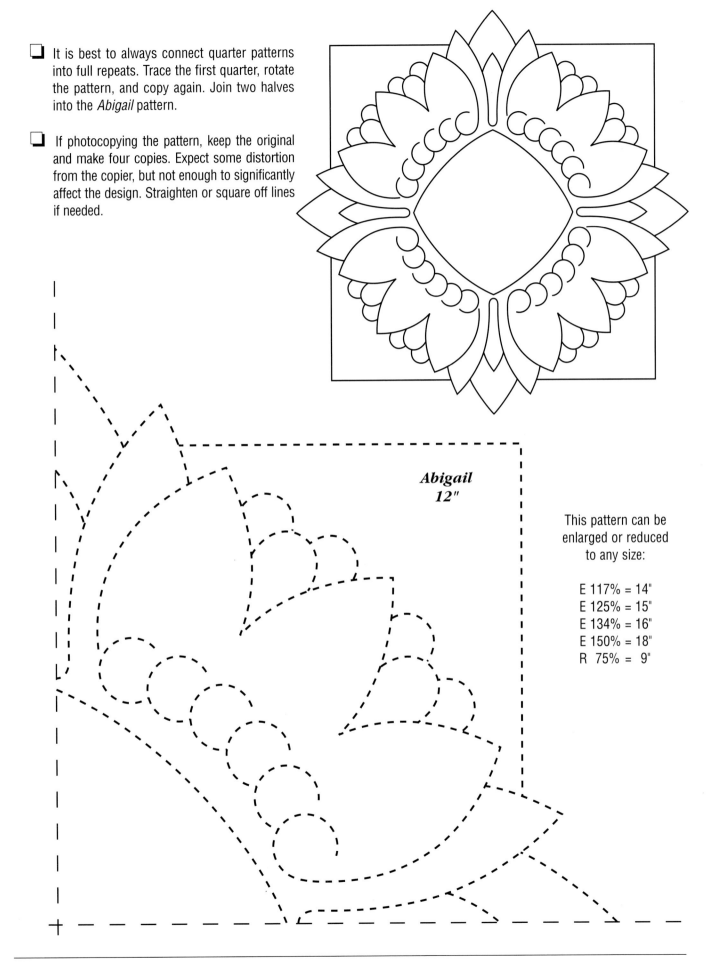

❑ It is best to always connect quarter patterns into full repeats. Trace the first quarter, rotate the pattern, and copy again. Join two halves into the *Abigail* pattern.

❑ If photocopying the pattern, keep the original and make four copies. Expect some distortion from the copier, but not enough to significantly affect the design. Straighten or square off lines if needed.

Abigail
12"

This pattern can be enlarged or reduced to any size:

E 117% = 14"
E 125% = 15"
E 134% = 16"
E 150% = 18"
R 75% = 9"

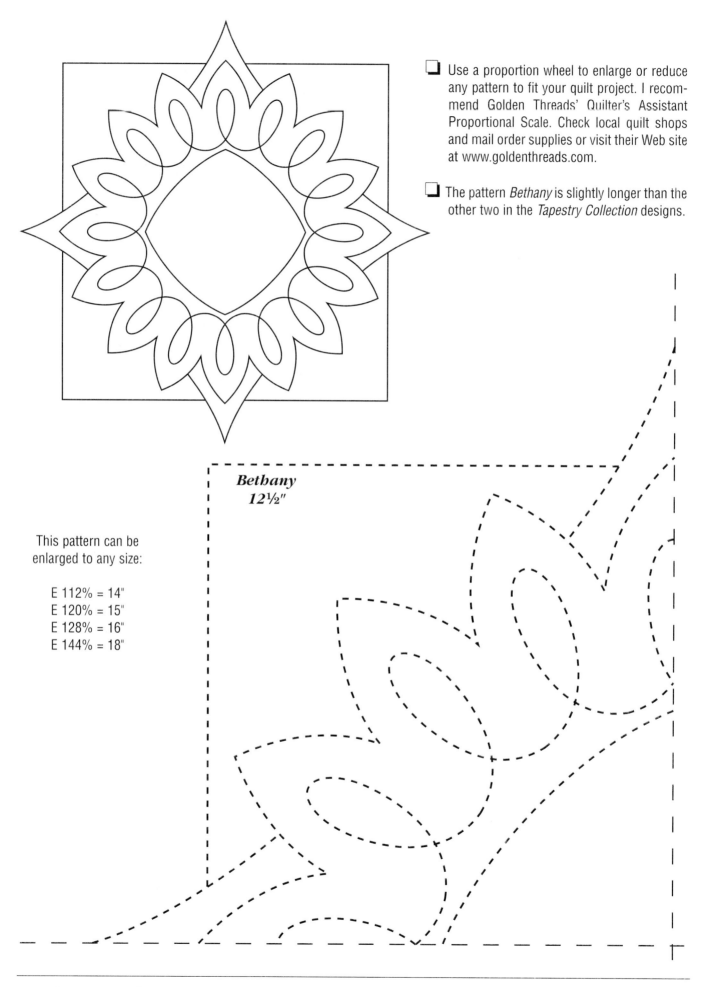

- Use a proportion wheel to enlarge or reduce any pattern to fit your quilt project. I recommend Golden Threads' Quilter's Assistant Proportional Scale. Check local quilt shops and mail order supplies or visit their Web site at www.goldenthreads.com.

- The pattern *Bethany* is slightly longer than the other two in the *Tapestry Collection* designs.

Bethany
12½"

This pattern can be enlarged to any size:

E 112% = 14"
E 120% = 15"
E 128% = 16"
E 144% = 18"

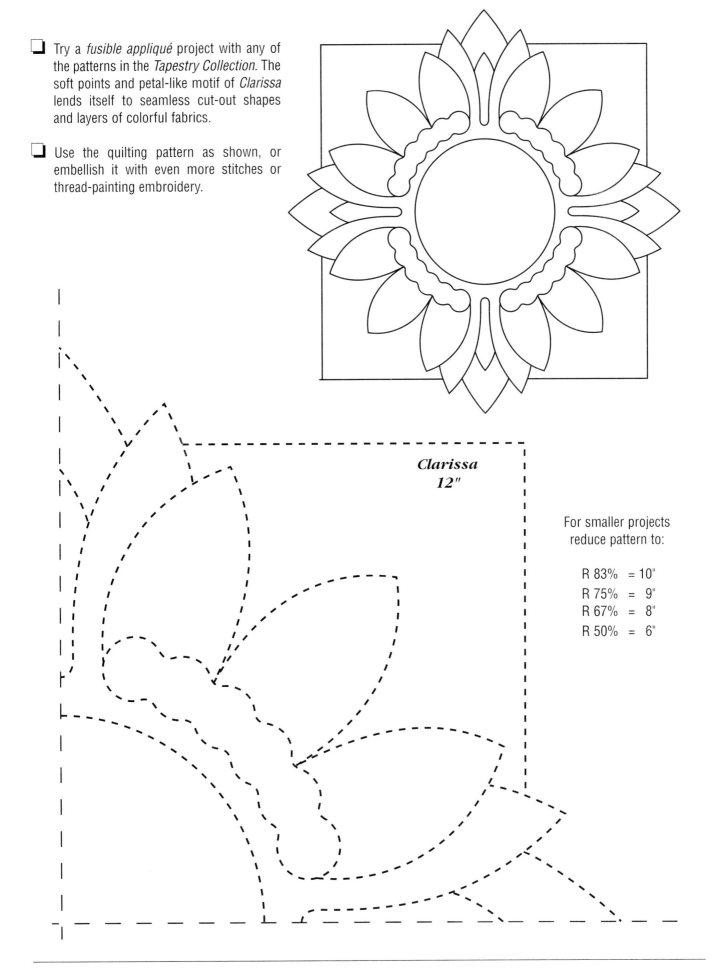

❏ Try a *fusible appliqué* project with any of the patterns in the *Tapestry Collection*. The soft points and petal-like motif of *Clarissa* lends itself to seamless cut-out shapes and layers of colorful fabrics.

❏ Use the quilting pattern as shown, or embellish it with even more stitches or thread-painting embroidery.

Clarissa
12"

For smaller projects reduce pattern to:

R 83% = 10"
R 75% = 9"
R 67% = 8"
R 50% = 6"

Secondary Design

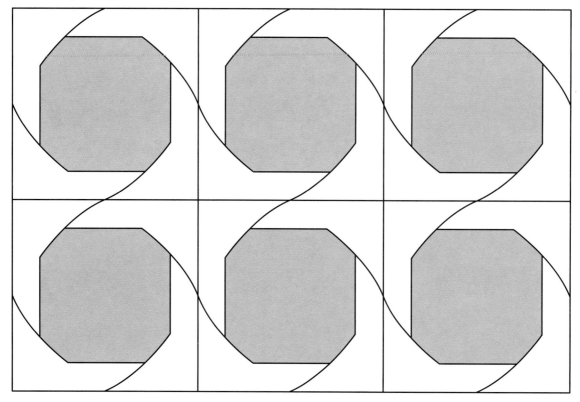

☐ Coloring in the negative space when you make a worksheet helps identify the area left unquilted. Depending on the batting requirements, more quilting might be needed.

☐ Appliqué or embroidered motifs would be framed by the *Woodbury* pattern while patchwork squares are divided into smaller sections. Outline quilt around any additions.

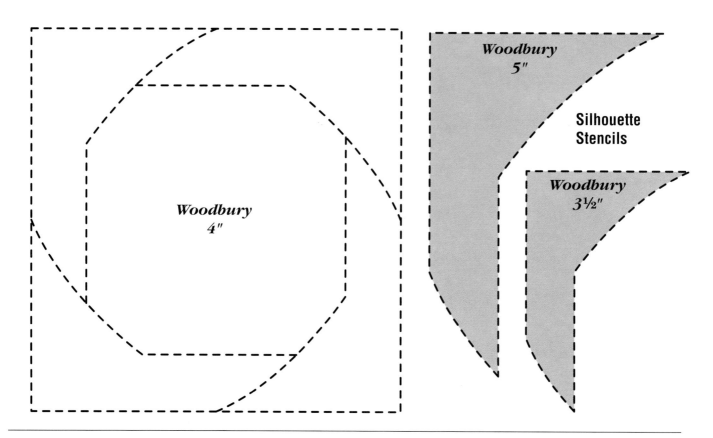

Woodbury
4"

Woodbury
5"

Silhouette Stencils

Woodbury
3½"

Chapter Three

Traditional Patterns

Utilizing Plastic Stencils with Preplanning

☐ A quilter since 1973, I was weaned on traditional quilt patterns with fine hand quilting, yet I now embrace designing patterns that can be marked and quilted in half the time. Try the *Heavenly Delight Series* (pages 34–40) with alternated hand and continuous patterns–and see for yourself how they can look the same after quilting.

☐ Quilters love hearts! Use *Sharon's Sweetheart* for blocks and sashing strips (pages 42–43) and *Patti's Cable* for borders. Especially lovely are its 2", 2½", 3", and 3½" sizes, popular for quilting on the sewing machine. See pages 44–46.

☐ Most of my patterns are available from Quilting Creations International (www.quiltingcreations.com) as plastic stencils. *Look for the HS number stamped in the corner. A slotted stencil is a wonderful *marking* tool that still requires *preplanning* prior to its use.

☐ If you prewash your fabric you will appreciate that preparation time pays dividends in the final quilt! Before you can start marking, you need to trace the design onto paper and reconnect the cut-out slots. This allows you to "see" the entire quilting design when planning.

☐ Next, make six extra copies – the larger the quilt, the more copies you need. Be sure to turn over the stencil and trace the reverse side too. Having copies of both sides is crucial for preplanning (even if you decide later not to use them).

☐ If the original pattern can be folded into something new, then the original stencil can be used to mark your quilt. Multiple copies (repeats) can be manipulated and folded to form single ❶ and double widths ❷; be reversed at center ❸; be mitered at corners ❹; cut apart into segments, and placed facing out ❺ or facing in ❻. They can also be used in block and corner triangles.

☐ The traditional *Celestial Cable* stencil was modified for continuous line. The feathers were omitted.

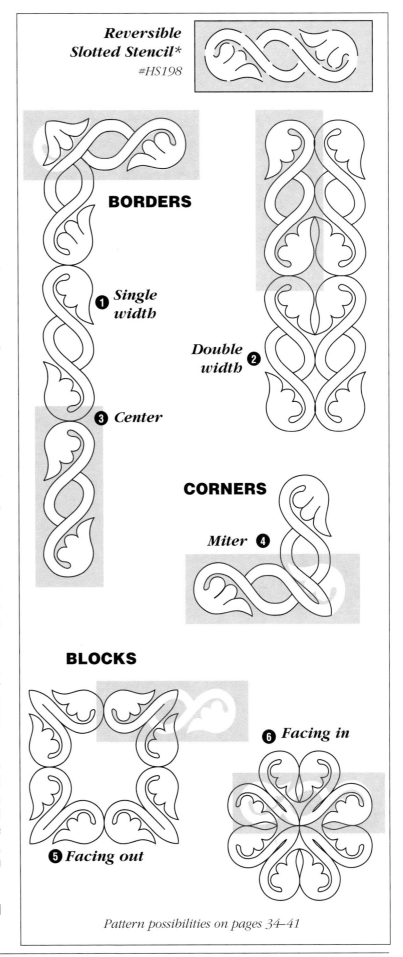

Reversible Slotted Stencil*
#HS198

BORDERS

❶ *Single width*

❷ *Double width*

❸ *Center*

CORNERS

Miter ❹

BLOCKS

❺ *Facing out*

❻ *Facing in*

Pattern possibilities on pages 34–41

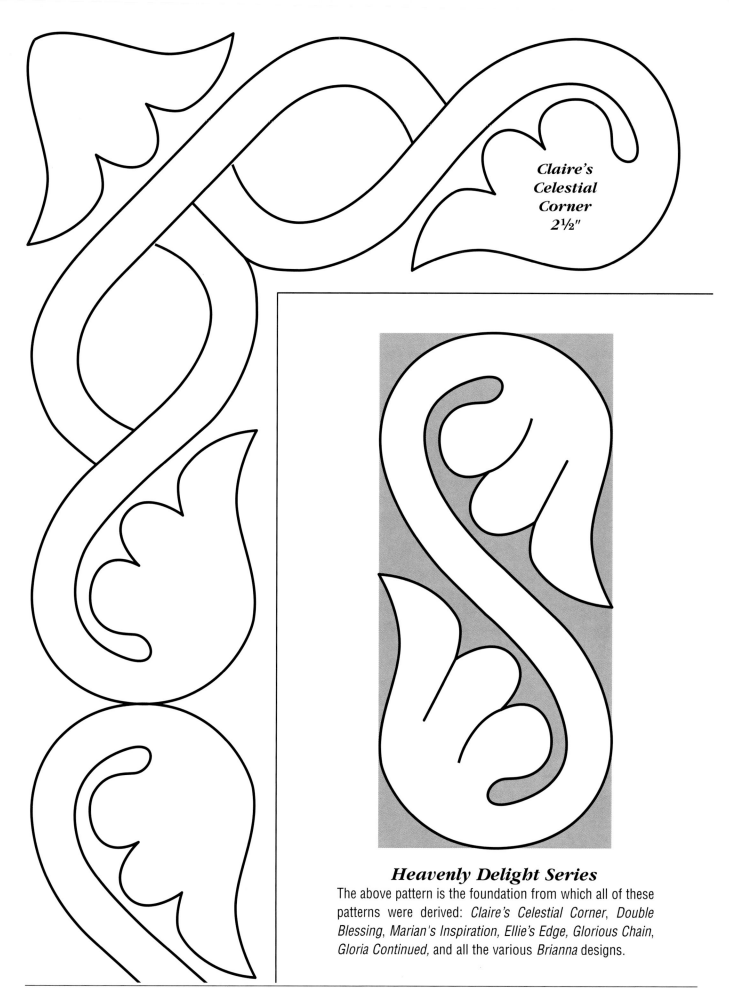

*Claire's
Celestial
Corner
2½"*

Heavenly Delight Series

The above pattern is the foundation from which all of these patterns were derived: *Claire's Celestial Corner, Double Blessing, Marian's Inspiration, Ellie's Edge, Glorious Chain, Gloria Continued,* and all the various *Brianna* designs.

Secondary Design – Sets of *Double Blessings* are reversed and touch horizontally. See page 98 for more possibilities.

Double Blessings 7"

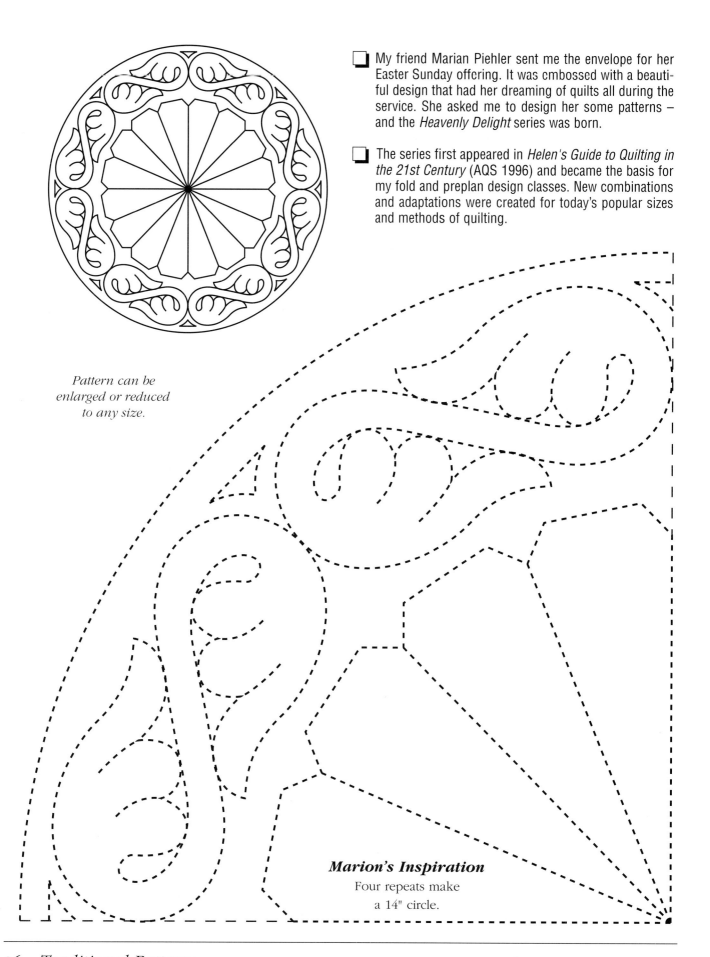

My friend Marian Piehler sent me the envelope for her Easter Sunday offering. It was embossed with a beautiful design that had her dreaming of quilts all during the service. She asked me to design her some patterns – and the *Heavenly Delight* series was born.

The series first appeared in *Helen's Guide to Quilting in the 21st Century* (AQS 1996) and became the basis for my fold and preplan design classes. New combinations and adaptations were created for today's popular sizes and methods of quilting.

Pattern can be enlarged or reduced to any size.

Marion's Inspiration
Four repeats make
a 14" circle.

From Hand to Machine

- The *Heavenly Delight* series is a combination of patterns for both hand and machine quilting. The simplest change was to eliminate the longer feathers between the motif while keeping the scooped and scalloped outline.

- *Finger trace* quilting patterns to determine where to start and stop. Remember that it is perfectly acceptable to double-up, or cover over, a previously stitched line when machine quilting. Keep stitches close, neat, and uniform in length.

- I have samples of both quilting styles using these patterns, and they appear very similar in the final designs.

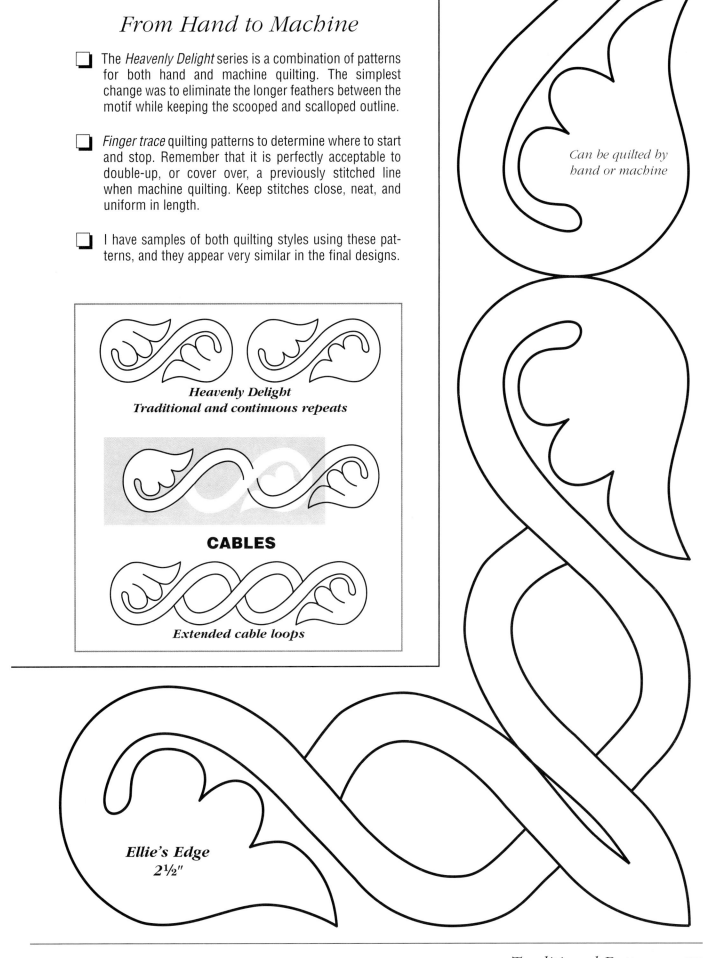

Can be quilted by hand or machine

Heavenly Delight
Traditional and continuous repeats

CABLES

Extended cable loops

Ellie's Edge
2½"

Placement Diagram – Refer to page 99 for another placement idea.

Glorious Chain
7"

Placement Diagram – Four repeats of *Gloria Continued* make this undulating block.

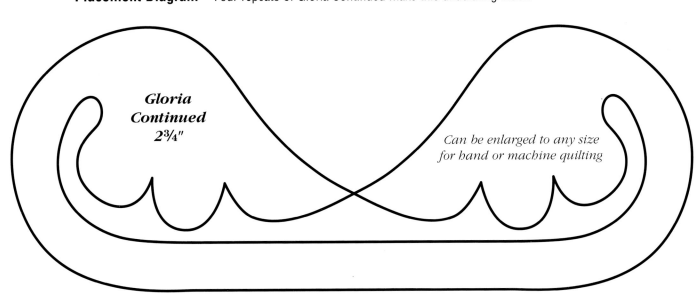

*Gloria
Continued
2¾"*

*Can be enlarged to any size
for hand or machine quilting*

Brianna's
Corner
2½"

Placement Diagram

☐ This part of the *Heavenly Delight Series* is named *Brianna*. It was made using two *Celestial Cables*, joined on top of each other and then folded in half width-wise (not shown).

☐ Once you make a new pattern, use extra copies and multiple repeats to create a new design like *Brianna's Corner*, above, and the mix-and-match sashing strip on page 41.

Brianna
4½"

Pattern can be
enlarged or reduced
to any size.

2"
Brianna Sashing

▼ Set square with minimum background.

▲ Set on-point requires a larger space.

Sharon's Corner & Border 4"

Sharon's Sweetheart 7"

Sharon Continuous 2" Sashing Strip

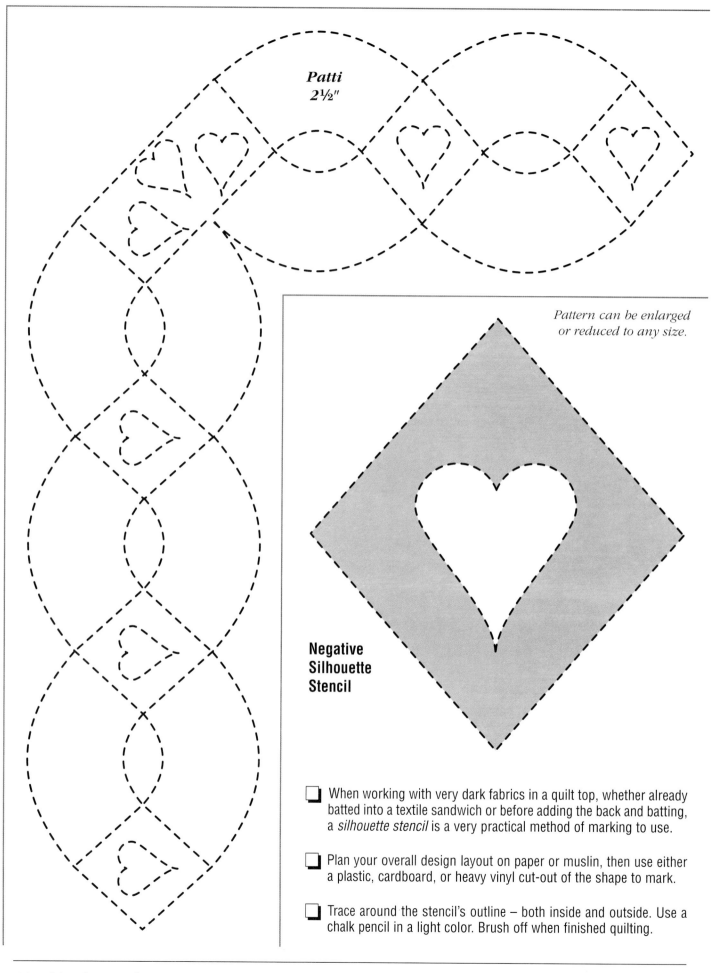

Patti
2½"

*Pattern can be enlarged
or reduced to any size.*

**Negative
Silhouette
Stencil**

☐ When working with very dark fabrics in a quilt top, whether already batted into a textile sandwich or before adding the back and batting, a *silhouette stencil* is a very practical method of marking to use.

☐ Plan your overall design layout on paper or muslin, then use either a plastic, cardboard, or heavy vinyl cut-out of the shape to mark.

☐ Trace around the stencil's outline – both inside and outside. Use a chalk pencil in a light color. Brush off when finished quilting.

Registration Marks

- [ ] Little icons of circles inside of crosshairs are called *registration marks*. They are used on some patterns to help identify the proper placement for the design. They are especially helpful for spacing odd shaped and asymmetrical patterns.

- [ ] Registration marks are excellent for repeated patterns. Simply match up the icons as you reposition the design or stencil. However, do *not* quilt them. They are only meant as guidelines.

- [ ] I like to think of them as representing grain lines and use them to help place my quilting patterns as I intended.

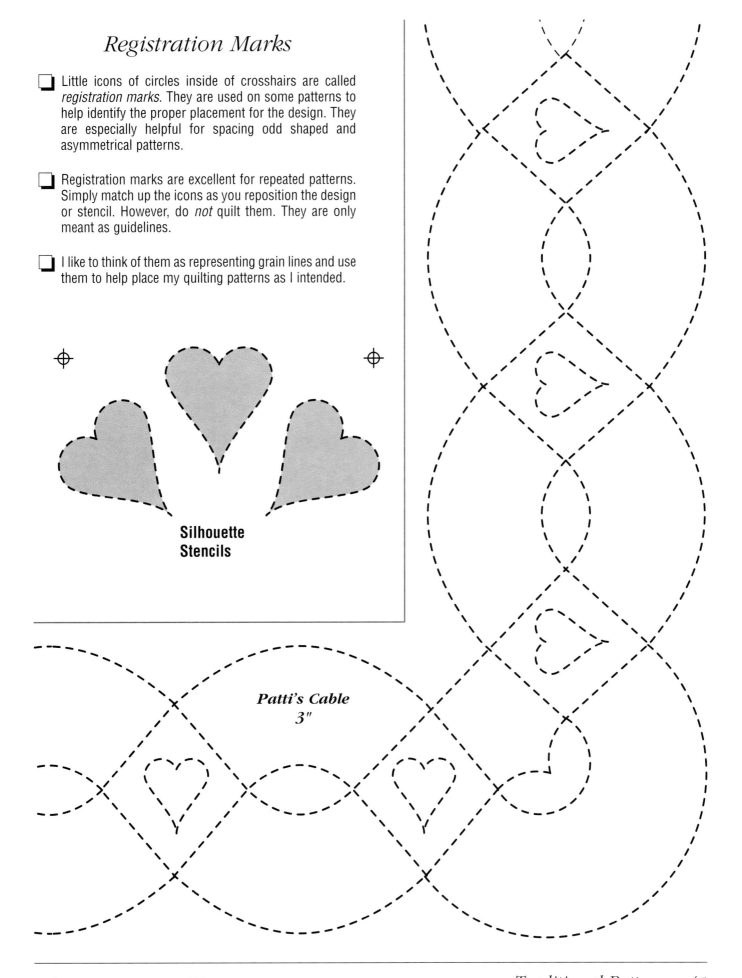

Silhouette Stencils

Patti's Cable 3"

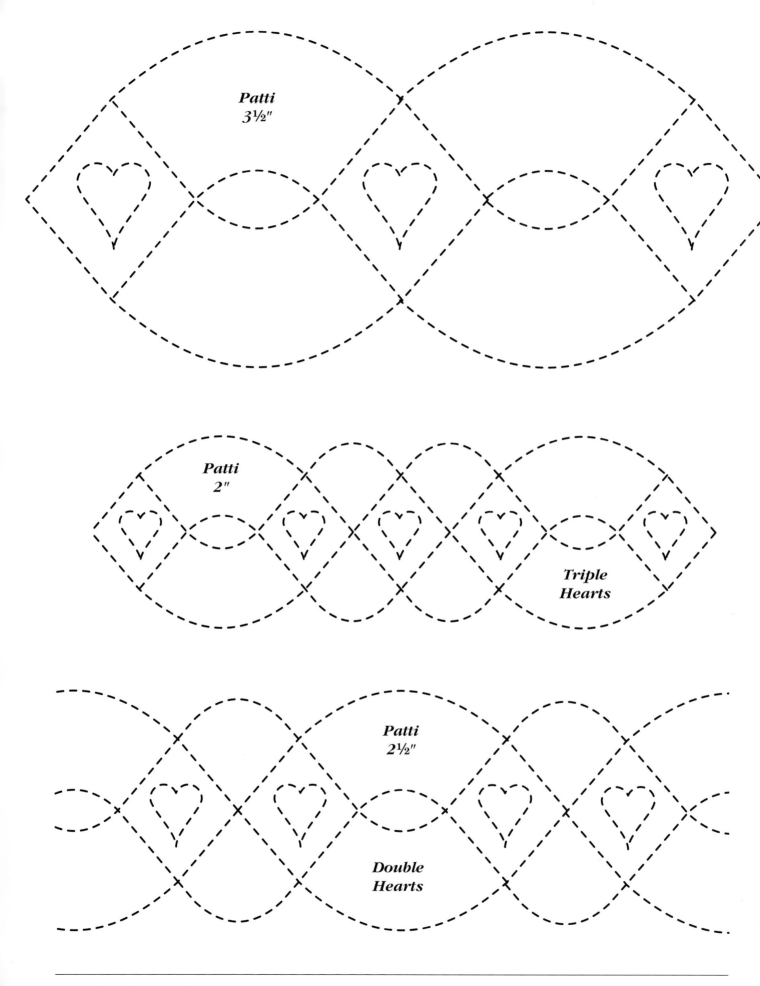

Patti
3½"

Patti
2"

Triple
Hearts

Patti
2½"

Double
Hearts

Make two copies.
Rotate to connect
repeats for full pattern.

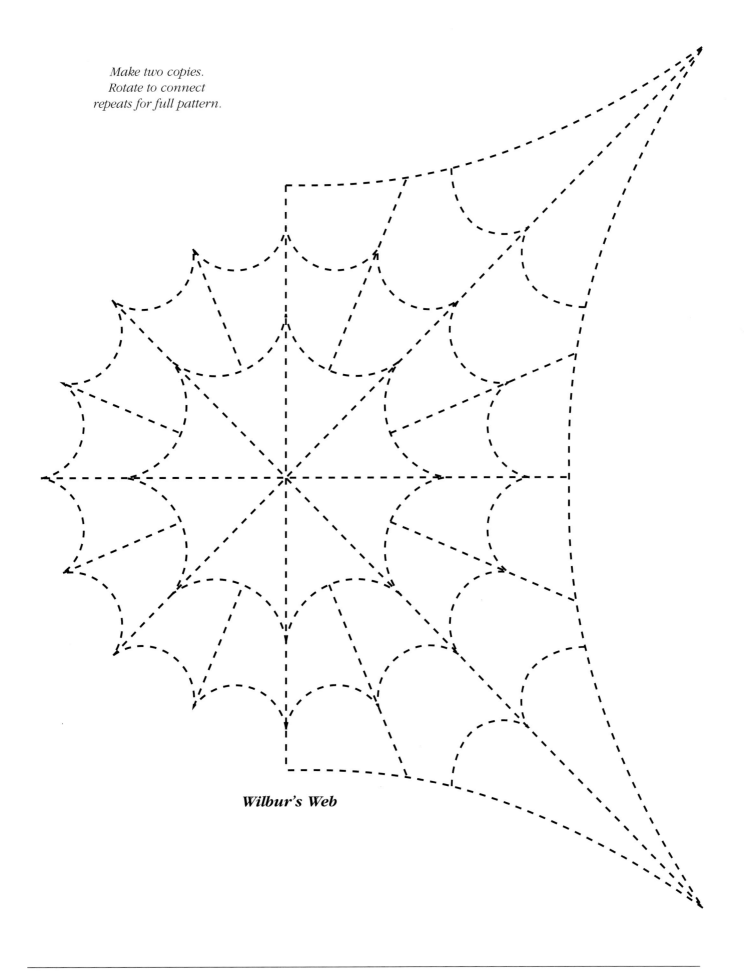

Wilbur's Web

Tapestry Medallion
7½"

Chapter Four

▶ *Continuous Lines*

☐ From free-motion machine sewing to edge-to-edge pantographs, the continuous-line patterns in the *Vine & Leaves Series* has something for everyone (pages 54–59).

☐ Learn more about *Muslin Master Patterns* (page 59) for planning and marking wholecloth quilts.

☐ Use the tips on page 60 to successfully *mix and match* elements when designing your own quilting patterns.

☐ The beautiful *Whitney* and its adaptation, *Kaylee,* are my favorite patterns in this book. See pages 62–66 for this series and chapter seven for their secondary designs.

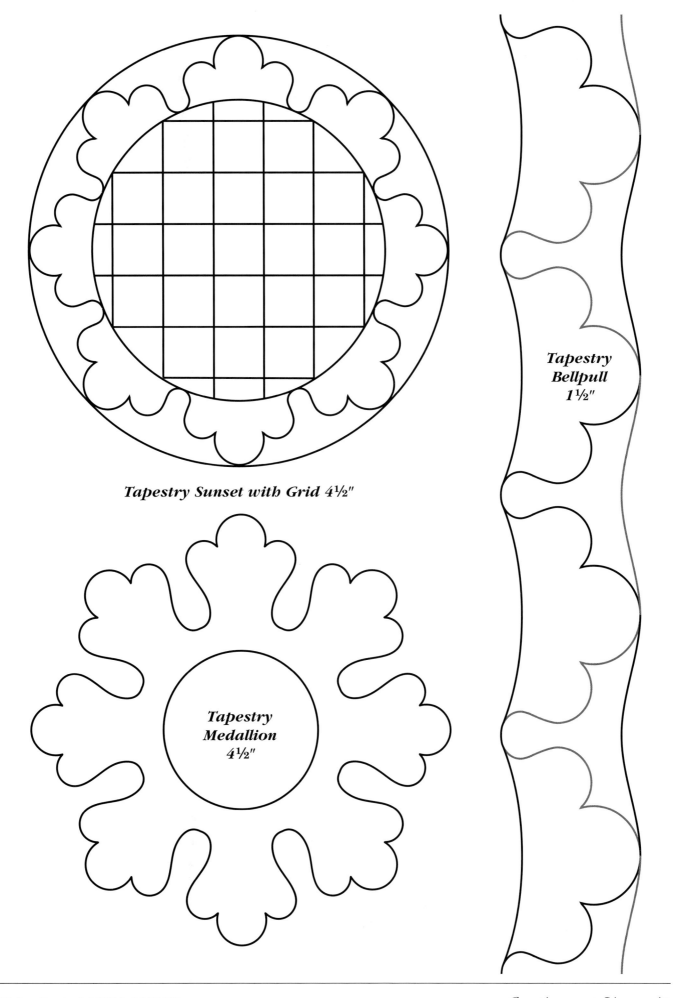

Tapestry Sunset with Grid 4½"

Tapestry Medallion 4½"

Tapestry Bellpull 1½"

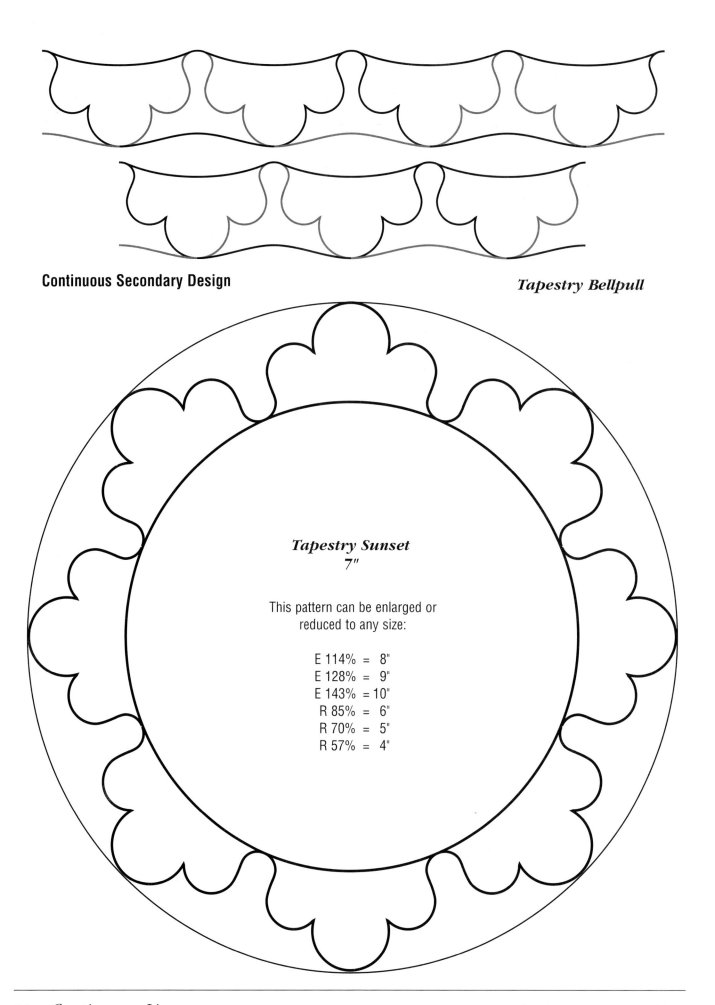

Continuous Secondary Design

Tapestry Bellpull

Tapestry Sunset
7"

This pattern can be enlarged or
reduced to any size:

E 114% = 8"
E 128% = 9"
E 143% = 10"
R 85% = 6"
R 70% = 5"
R 57% = 4"

Belle
4"

Patterns can be enlarge or reduced to any size
and can be quilted by hand or machine.

**Tapestry
Bellpull 2"**

Luminere
4"

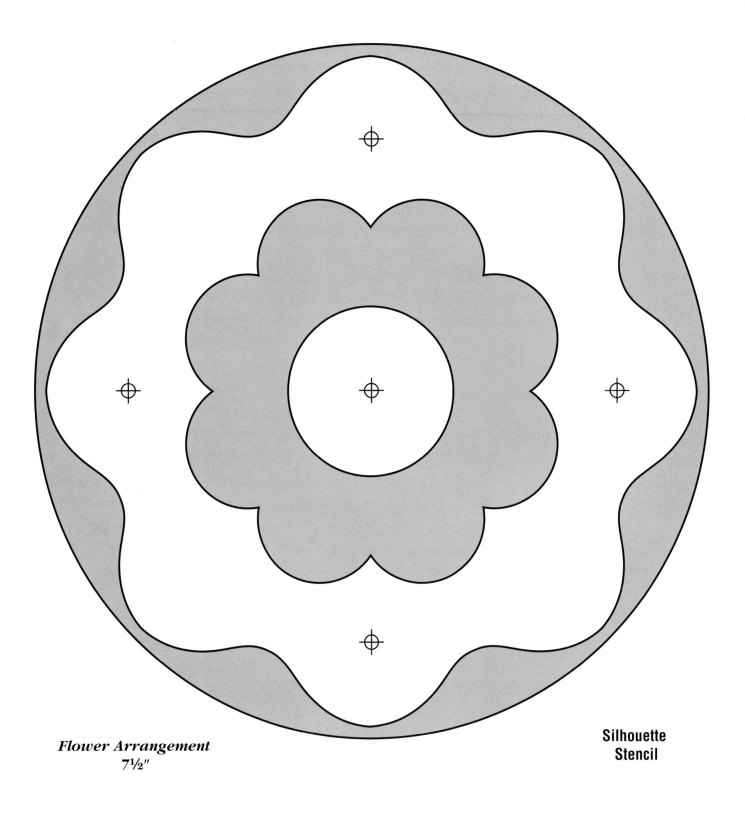

Flower Arrangement
7½"

**Silhouette
Stencil**

☐ It is easy to simplify and combine key elements in a variety of sizes in your projects.

☐ Trace the pattern onto cardboard or manila file folders, and carefully cut the undulating shapes apart.

☐ Maintaining the essence of the design – in this series a folk art feeling – gives continuity and unifies the patterns.

☐ Use these silhouette stencils to mark pre-batted quilts. Refer to the entire pattern for accurate placements.

Placement Diagram

☐ Over 80% of the quilts we make are rectangular in shape.

☐ Recognize rectangles and start a collection for future reference and use.

Thai Continuous Flower & Leaves 2"

For more in the series refer to page 101.

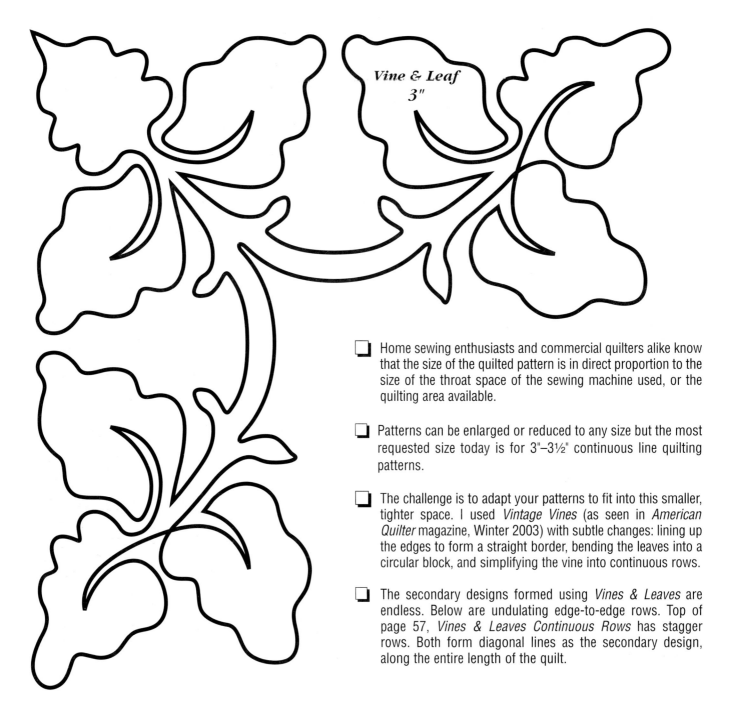

Vine & Leaf
3"

❑ Home sewing enthusiasts and commercial quilters alike know that the size of the quilted pattern is in direct proportion to the size of the throat space of the sewing machine used, or the quilting area available.

❑ Patterns can be enlarged or reduced to any size but the most requested size today is for 3"–3½" continuous line quilting patterns.

❑ The challenge is to adapt your patterns to fit into this smaller, tighter space. I used *Vintage Vines* (as seen in *American Quilter* magazine, Winter 2003) with subtle changes: lining up the edges to form a straight border, bending the leaves into a circular block, and simplifying the vine into continuous rows.

❑ The secondary designs formed using *Vines & Leaves* are endless. Below are undulating edge-to-edge rows. Top of page 57, *Vines & Leaves Continuous Rows* has stagger rows. Both form diagonal lines as the secondary design, along the entire length of the quilt.

Secondary Design

Secondary Design – Mitered squres with inner block of the *Vine & Leaf* pattern.

Vines & Leaves Edge-to-Edge

Tree
Trunks
5"

Vine & Leaf 2"

Vines & Leaves Continuous Rows

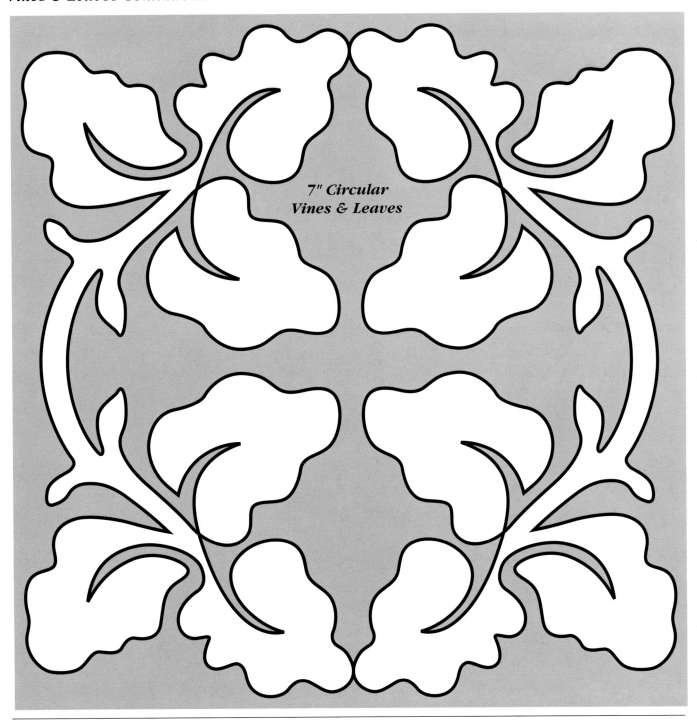

7" Circular
Vines & Leaves

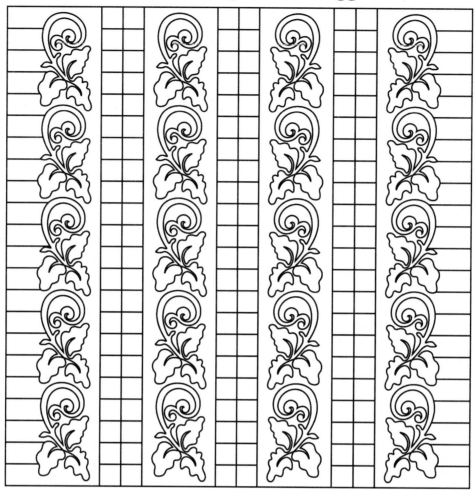

Stacked Strip Repeats – Rows reversed from the center

Serpentine Curves – Flopped and facing in one direction

Reversed Connections – Repeating reversed pairs

Undulating Curves – Flopped and reversed at center

Muslin Master Pattern

- [ ] By drafting the entire pattern on muslin first, it is easier to trace and mark the lines on the good fabric. The four-patches (shown in the illustration on page 58) can be pieced or just quilted in straight lines.

- [ ] Plan for one-quarter of the design layout plus a 2" overlap which allows you to see if the pattern is to be flipped, flopped, rotated, or reversed at the center of the quilt, etc.

- [ ] Draw the quilting design on the muslin with a fine line indelible black marker.

- [ ] Pin light-colored quilt fabric on top of the muslin. Trace the entire design with a regular color-matched chalk pencil. The muslin master pattern can be saved and used again.

- [ ] An underneath light source, such as a light box, sliding glass door, or glass-top coffee table makes tracing easier (shown below). Keryn Emmerson cautions that the heat of the glass may inadvertently set the ink markings.

Vintage Vine

*Actual pattern size –
make six copies as shown
and six reversed copies
to plan layout.*

Frame	+	Design	+	Grid	=	Pattern

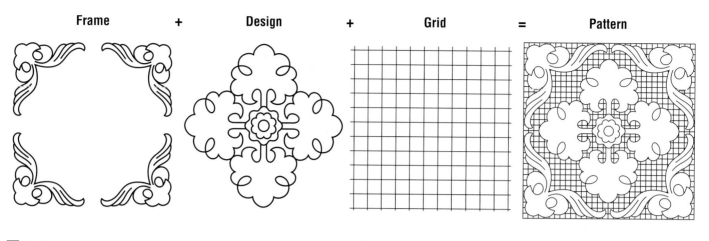

☐ Divide the background into smaller segments. Add or omit details.

☐ Select and showcase main motif. Enlarge or reduce to fit in frame.

☐ Flatten the background area with fillers of geometric gridlines.

☐ The combined patterns can be used to create secondary designs.

p. 76

p. 12

p. 102

p. 101

p. 61

p. 9

p. 73

p. 96

p. 36

Mix & Match Elements

❏ To use one-quarter patterns effectively you need five copies. Keep the original, and cut and join the four pieces into two halves, and then the whole repeat.

❏ The flower motif shown on page 52 was the basis for this *Tapestry Medallion* design. Experiment with combining elements from different patterns – mix and match the designs until you find the winning combination.

❏ Refer to the step-by-step illustration on the opposite page for a suggestion on using the *Winterthur Medallion* and the *Winterthur Scroll* (page 85).

❏ See About the Author on page 111 for the *Winterthur Table Runner* using multiple repeats.

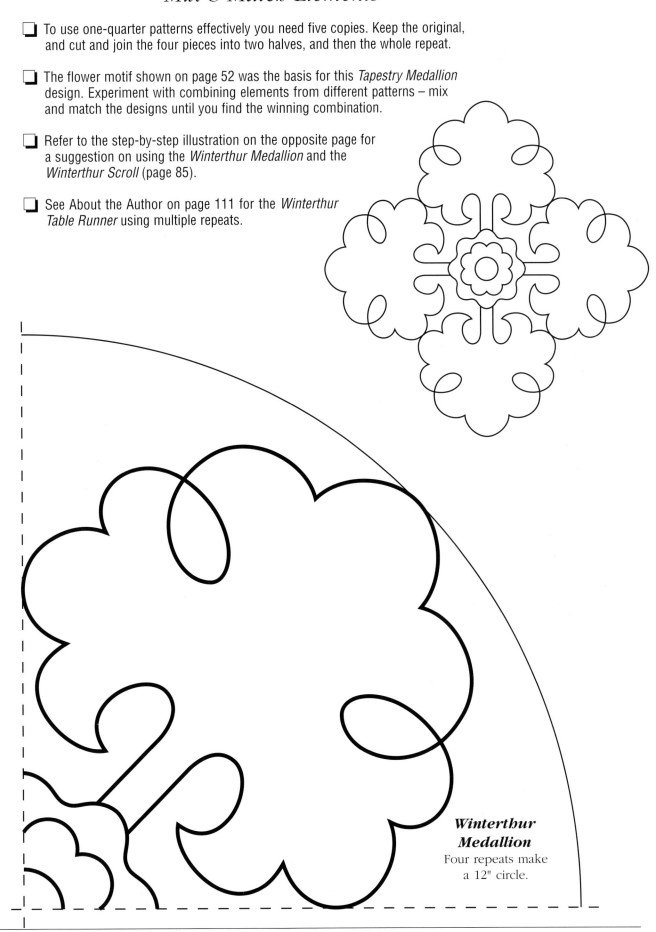

Winterthur Medallion
Four repeats make a 12" circle.

Whitney
9½"

☐ The sculptural appeal of *Whitney* can be further emphasized when trapunto (a soft stuffing or extra batting) is added behind the design motifs with water-soluble thread before the final quilting.

☐ Refer to chapter seven *Secondary Designs* (page 106) for a surprisingly contemporary look for this very traditional pattern.

4" x 19" **3½" x 16½"** **3" x 14"** **2½" x 12"** **2" x 9½"**

*Kaylee's
Border Design*

☐ Patterns can be enlarged by width ↕ (height) or by length ↔. Once you get the approximate size, it's time to adapt and adjust the pattern.

☐ Make at least six copies of the pattern and play with the layout; miter the corner, overlap repeats, and/or reverse the design at the center of the quilt.

☐ Plan for one quarter of the quilt plus a 2" overlap. This diagram shows that *Kaylee's Border Design* is rotated around all four sides. Additional repeats can be inserted as needed to fit your individual quilt size.

Placement Diagram

Kaylee
2"

Kaylee
4"

**Kaylee
Continuous Medallion**
7" x 7½"

This pattern can be
enlarged to any size:

E 114% = 8" x 8⁹⁄₁₆"
E 128% = 9" x 9⁵⁄₈"
E 143% = 10" x 10¾"
E 171% = 12" x 12⅞"

**Kaylee's
Korner**
2"

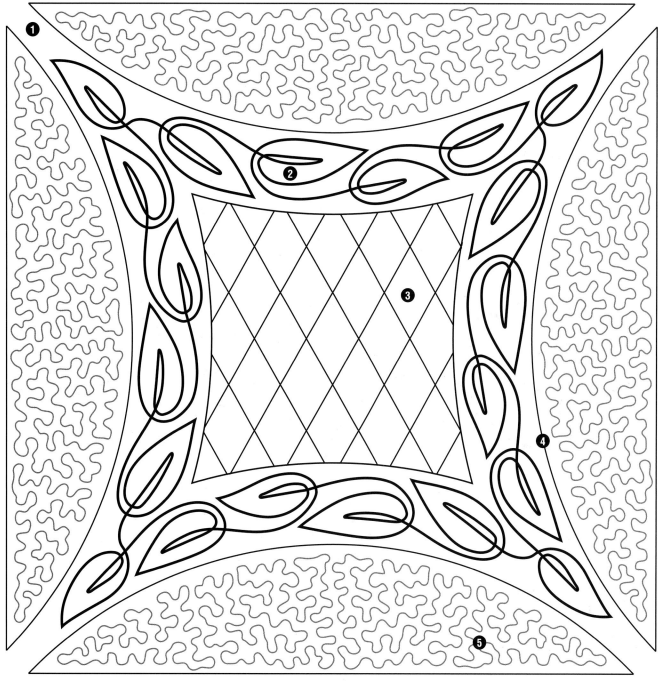

Mary's Meandering Leaves Variation 7"

In chapter one, *More Helen's Hints*, the quilt top on page 10 is typical of those brought to my UFOs class. The flowing lines of *Mary's Meandering Leaves Variation* (above) is the type of quilting design that shows off the patchwork while camouflaging the mismatched seams.

Be prepared to adjust the length and width of the Robbing Peter to Pay Paul template ❶ to compensate for the irregular sizes of the original blocks.

The design motif ❷ should complement the patchwork blocks and the proportion needs to fit in the bigger plain blocks. They measure anywhere between 14½"–15½".

Do *not* change the size of the diamond gridlines ❸. They should remain the same even if you elongate or stretch the surrounding Robbing Peter to Pay Paul template.

The soft curves ❹ that surround the patchwork blocks showcase the vivid colors and the *Mother's Choice* pattern (refer to page 11).

A meandering fill ❺ will flatten the background between the circular quilting design and the patchwork pattern. The irregular piecing (cut-off triangles) will be less noticeable.

Trace, scan, or photocopy then enlarge or reduced to any size.

**J.W.'s
Rose Spray**

Jane Winter Price's Design
Continuous

☐ To adapt a pattern from hand quilting to continuous you need to finger trace the main pattern. In *Jane Winter Price's Design* the flower and stem are separated into units that can be placed in a triangle or used as individual pieces/patterns.

Toula's Twirl

☐ For a full circular pattern, make four copies and rotate each, then connect repeats. Registration marks are usually provided for offset or tilted patterns. The circle icon indicates placement in relation to the grain of the fabric.

☐ To stack repeats for pantographs, scan or trace, and reverse the pattern. It can then be enlarged or reduced to any size. Refer to pages 7–9 for more placement suggestions using *Toula's Twirl*.

Secondary Design

Alisson
7"

Chapter Five

Beautiful Scrolls

- My personal style of quilting glorifies swirls and curls in traditional-looking quilts. My designs appeal to today's quilters because they can be hand or machine quilted.

- My truly good friend, Joyce Lockatell, has her namesake patterns revised as corners, blocks, and quilts – all perfect for trapunto – on pages 78–81.

- The elegant *Winterthur Scroll* (page 85) is a recurring element throughout the book. See About the Author, page 111, for the coordinating table runner.

- The cover quilt pattern is showcased in a variety of sizes, in silhouette stencils and, in its main attraction, *McTavish,* on pages 86–89.

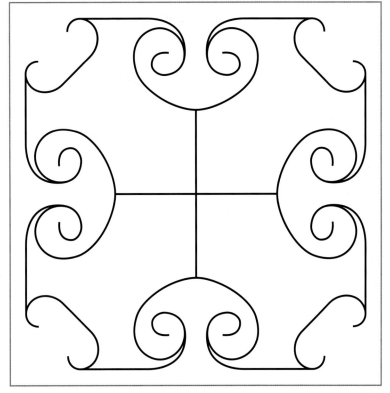

Denise
4"

Charlotte
4"

◀ *Charlotte Sashing 2"*

Paducah Scrollwork 6½"

Paducah, Kentucky

*

❏ There are plenty of pattern ideas in historic and architecturally enhanced buildings. From carved wooden porches to filigree street lights, design ideas surround us wherever we live – we only need to look! A cast-iron plant stand inspired this Paducah series.

❏ Notice how the simple act of overlapping scroll lines in different directions (✱) can create an entirely new shape.

❏ An enlarged pattern can be autographed and used as a *souvenir block*.

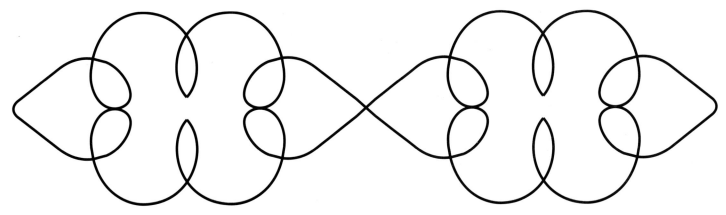

Continuous Puzzle Pieces 2"

Paducah Puzzle 7"

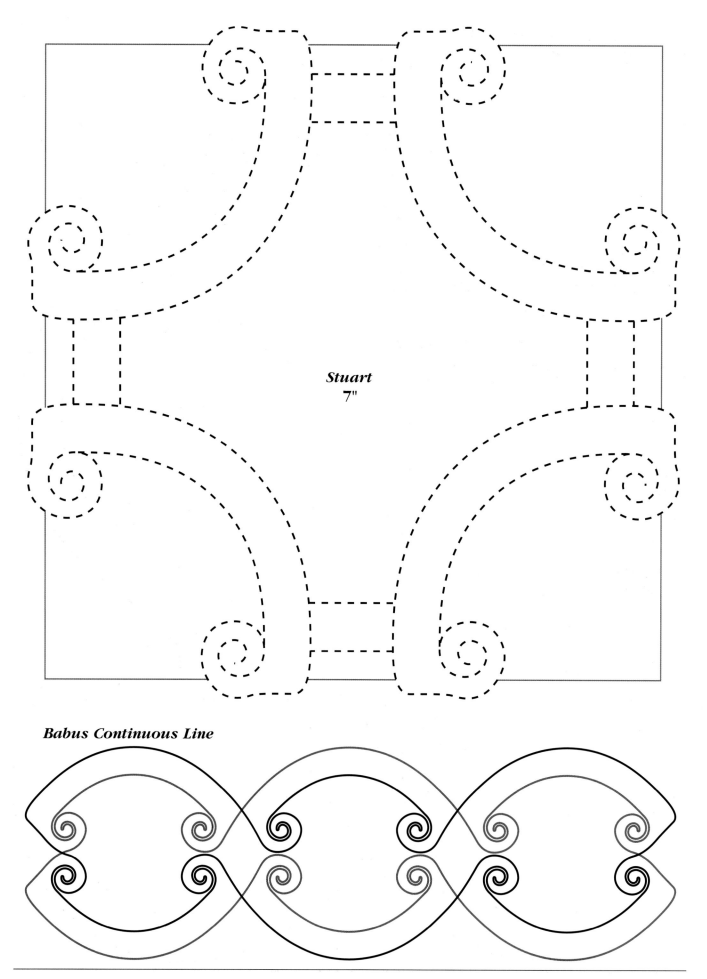

Stuart
7"

Babus Continuous Line

▲ Divide the border and have scallops facing inward,

Placement Diagrams

▼ or, use the other half of the border facing outward.

Babus Border
3½"

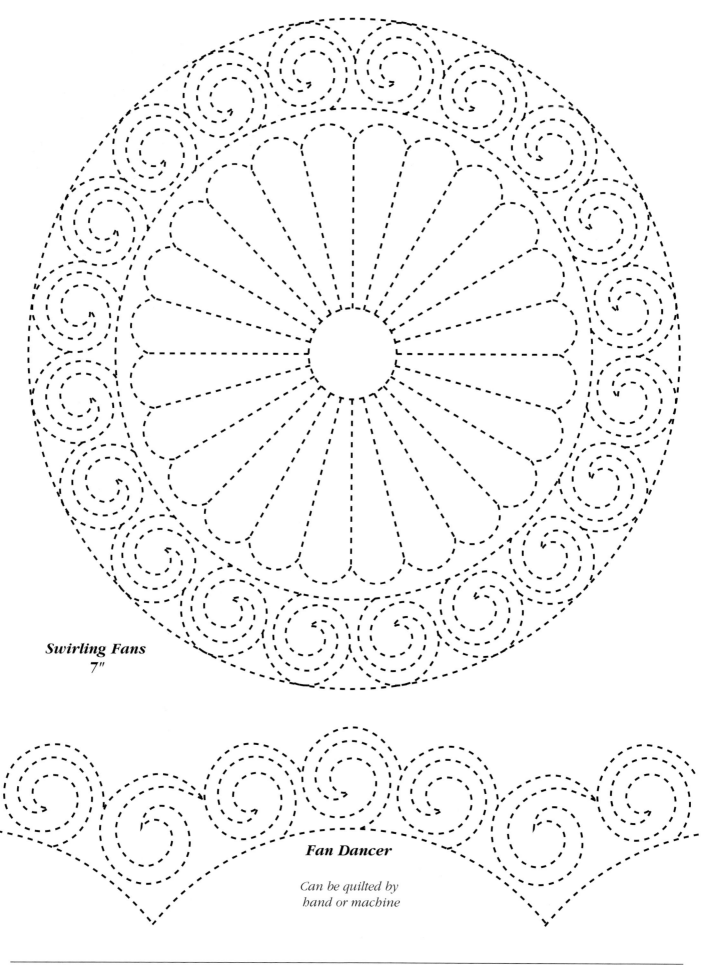

Swirling Fans
7"

Fan Dancer

*Can be quilted by
hand or machine*

Curved lines needed to form circular patterns look better when combined with linear lines. See how the traditional Dresden Plate pattern gives balance to the intricate design *Swirling Fans*.

Another designer trick is to combine odd and even elements. A repeat of five swirls with six petals (per quarter section) adds variety and eye appeal.

Trace one quarter.

Rotate pattern and copy again.

Join two halves into a full circle.

Swirling Fans
Four repeats make
a 14" circle.

Secondary Design – To create *Theresa Joyce*, reverse full-size pattern and add additional crown details.

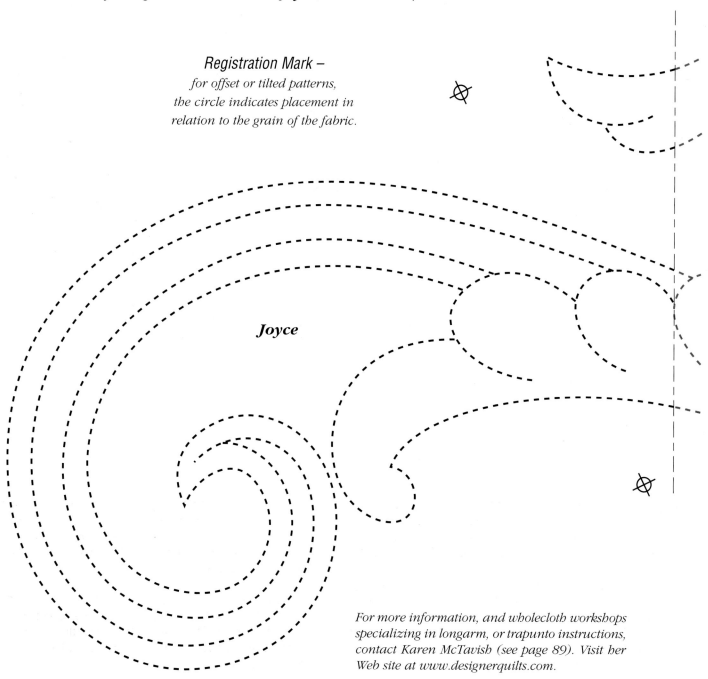

Registration Mark –
for offset or tilted patterns,
the circle indicates placement in
relation to the grain of the fabric.

Joyce

For more information, and wholecloth workshops
specializing in longarm, or trapunto instructions,
contact Karen McTavish (see page 89). Visit her
Web site at www.designerquilts.com.

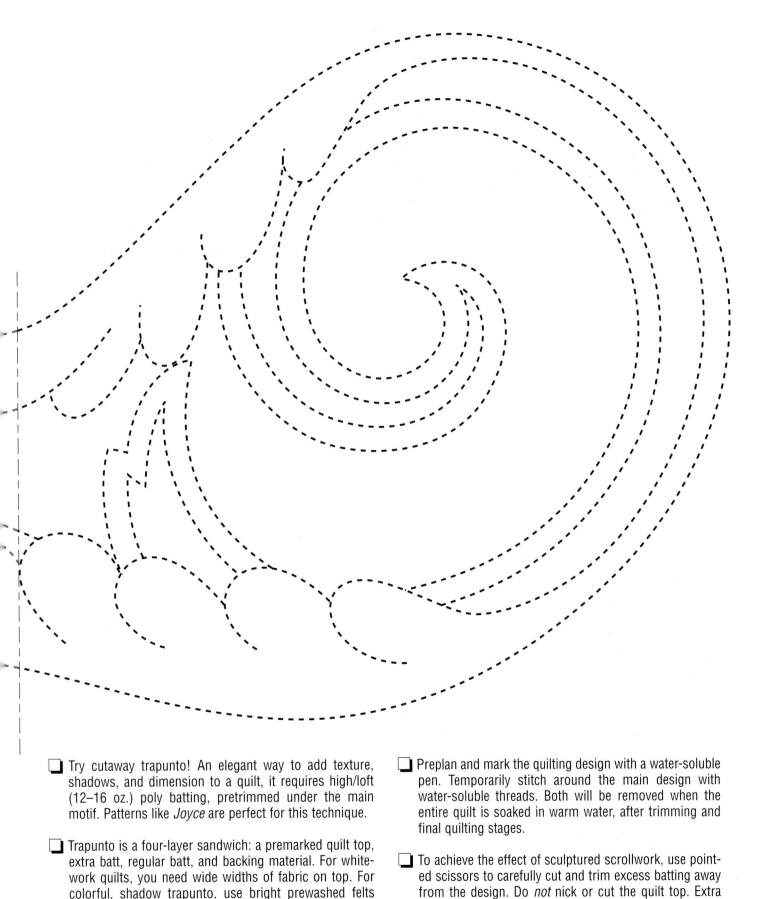

☐ Try cutaway trapunto! An elegant way to add texture, shadows, and dimension to a quilt, it requires high/loft (12–16 oz.) poly batting, pretrimmed under the main motif. Patterns like *Joyce* are perfect for this technique.

☐ Trapunto is a four-layer sandwich: a premarked quilt top, extra batt, regular batt, and backing material. For whitework quilts, you need wide widths of fabric on top. For colorful, shadow trapunto, use bright prewashed felts and flannels which will appear as pastels when placed underneath translucent, sheer fabrics.

☐ Preplan and mark the quilting design with a water-soluble pen. Temporarily stitch around the main design with water-soluble threads. Both will be removed when the entire quilt is soaked in warm water, after trimming and final quilting stages.

☐ To achieve the effect of sculptured scrollwork, use pointed scissors to carefully cut and trim excess batting away from the design. Do *not* nick or cut the quilt top. Extra details can be added inside the design later when the layers are quilted again.

Secondary Design – Use background fillers of crosshatching and micro-stippling (shown shaded) to make the scrollwork pattern *Theresa Joyce* pop out.

Lockatell Links

Joyce
Modified Corner

☐ The original pattern *Joyce* (pages 78–79) was duplicated and mitered at the corner. Certain modifications were then made to simplify the design for quilting.

☐ In *Joyce's Modified Corner* there is only one row of double stitches, and the outside curve line has been foreshortened. It can still be marked with the original *Joyce* stencil.

Placement Diagram

Placement Diagram

☐ Make two copies, one a reverse, and connect repeats for the full *Lynette* pattern. If wanted, nestle and add *Madaline* side pieces as shown above.

Lynette
Traditional

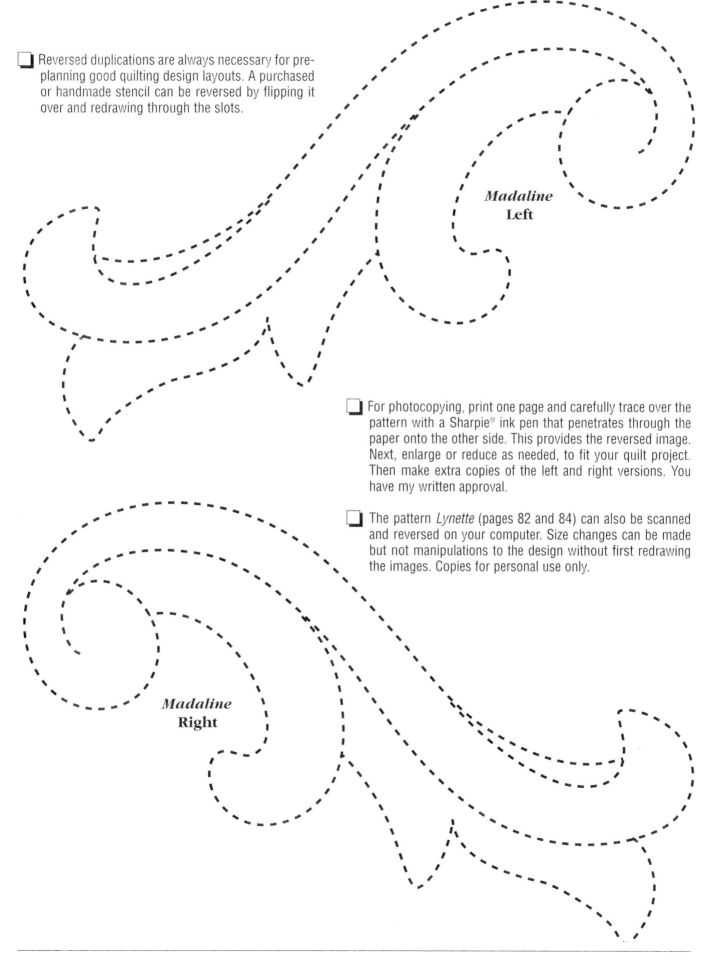

❏ Reversed duplications are always necessary for pre-planning good quilting design layouts. A purchased or handmade stencil can be reversed by flipping it over and redrawing through the slots.

Madaline
Left

❏ For photocopying, print one page and carefully trace over the pattern with a Sharpie® ink pen that penetrates through the paper onto the other side. This provides the reversed image. Next, enlarge or reduce as needed, to fit your quilt project. Then make extra copies of the left and right versions. You have my written approval.

❏ The pattern *Lynette* (pages 82 and 84) can also be scanned and reversed on your computer. Size changes can be made but not manipulations to the design without first redrawing the images. Copies for personal use only.

Madaline
Right

Placement Diagram

*Make two copies,
one a reverse, to connect
repeats for the full pattern.*

Lynette
Continuous

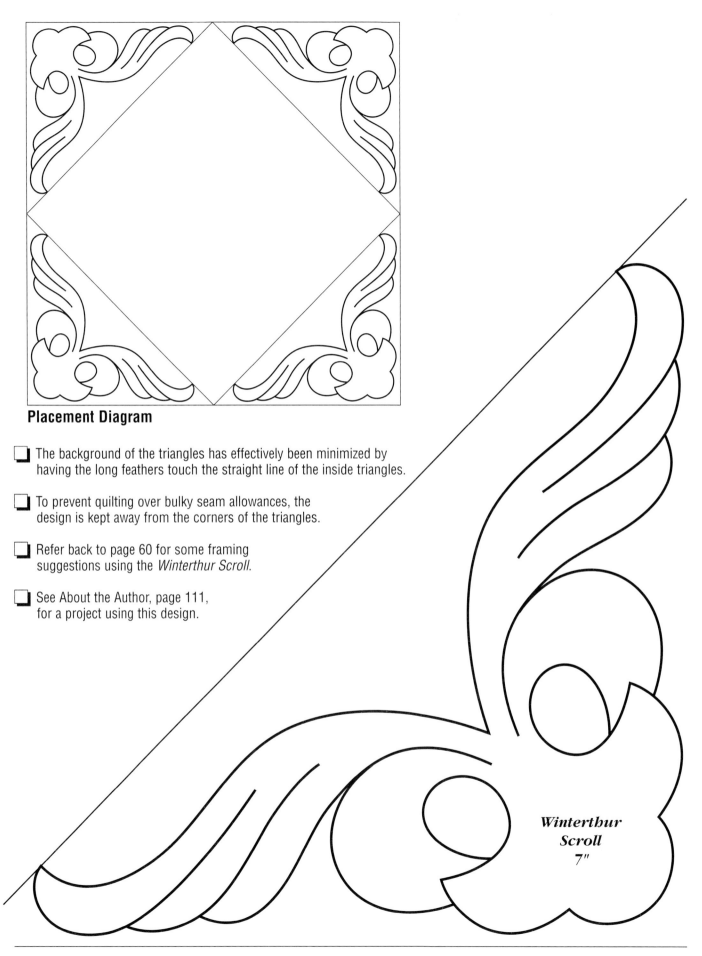

Placement Diagram

- [ ] The background of the triangles has effectively been minimized by having the long feathers touch the straight line of the inside triangles.

- [ ] To prevent quilting over bulky seam allowances, the design is kept away from the corners of the triangles.

- [ ] Refer back to page 60 for some framing suggestions using the *Winterthur Scroll*.

- [ ] See About the Author, page 111, for a project using this design.

Winterthur Scroll 7"

Silhouette
Stencil

McTavish

McTavish Border
Left

McTavish Center

Silhouette Stencil

McTavish Border Right

◀ Four alternated repeats

McTavish
4" x 9"

Placement Diagram – A heart forms when the center is reversed at an angle – a perfect design for trapunto!

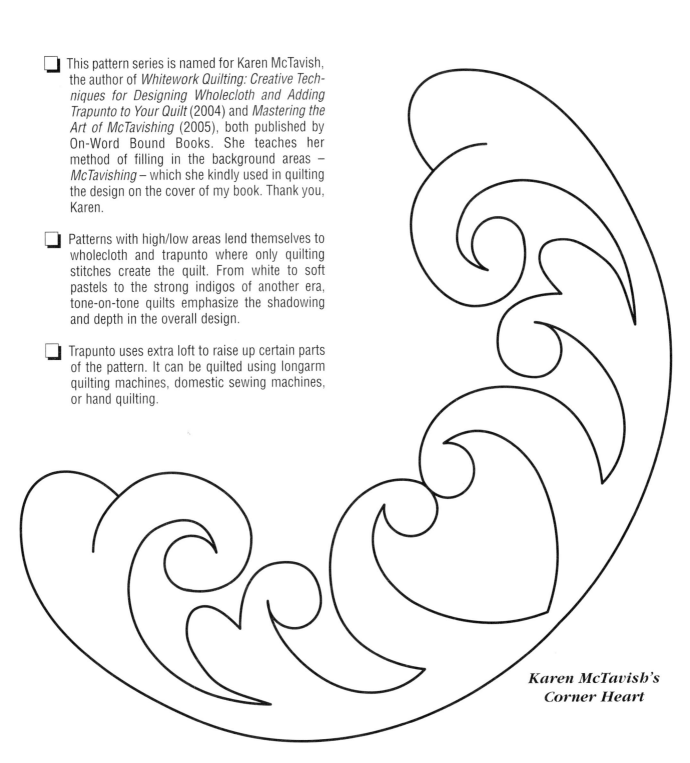

☐ This pattern series is named for Karen McTavish, the author of *Whitework Quilting: Creative Techniques for Designing Wholecloth and Adding Trapunto to Your Quilt* (2004) and *Mastering the Art of McTavishing* (2005), both published by On-Word Bound Books. She teaches her method of filling in the background areas – *McTavishing* – which she kindly used in quilting the design on the cover of my book. Thank you, Karen.

☐ Patterns with high/low areas lend themselves to wholecloth and trapunto where only quilting stitches create the quilt. From white to soft pastels to the strong indigos of another era, tone-on-tone quilts emphasize the shadowing and depth in the overall design.

☐ Trapunto uses extra loft to raise up certain parts of the pattern. It can be quilted using longarm quilting machines, domestic sewing machines, or hand quilting.

Karen McTavish's
Corner Heart

Chapter Six

▶ *Grids VII*

☐ To use grid lines, first design and plan for one-fourth of the quilt's layout plus a 2" overlap ❶ that shows if the pattern will be rotated, revised at the center, mitered at the corners, etc. For quilts under 45" in width, make a full-size, complete layout. It's easier to accurately trace onto the good fabric (see *Muslin Master Pattern*, page 59) when the muslin does not have to be repositioned.

☐ Mark on muslin (inexpensive cotton fabric) with a fine-line editable black ink pen to create a permanent pattern that is durable, does not rip, is easy to store, and is reusable. The grid lines are slipped *under* the muslin after the design motifs have been placed in position ❷ and traced. Refer to your worksheet on page 8.

☐ All seven of the *Dear Helen* series have a chapter with predrawn grid lines. Usually two pages of the same size grid can be connected together (see pages 92–95) to give a larger work surface.

☐ My Weight Watchers® theory is to add or take away five pounds wherever necessary! When grid lines hit the design motif in awkward spots ❸ change the motif by *adding* wider curves or *reducing* the shape.

☐ The open area of the hearts was used to experiment with crosshatching. I tried both ½" and 1" grid lines ❹ and also marked different placement possibilities inside each area. The one that looked the best was then used to mark all the hearts alike. The quilt CUPID'S HEART was featured in *Helen's Copy & Use Quilting Patterns* (AQS 2002).

☐ Note the two short lines drawn through any wrong lines made by either a slipped ruler or by a change of mind. These notations ❺ of mistakes and crooked lines can be quickly avoided and omitted later when you mark your good lines on the quilt top with a chalk pencil, and a water-erasable, or water-soluble pretested pen.

☐ Grids are mathematical measurements that do not change. Photocopies will distort their accuracy so it is better to use tracings, or pages of scanned grid lines, when planning your quilt.

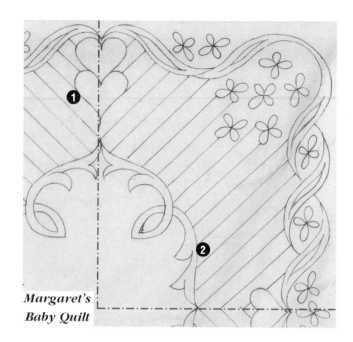

Margaret's Baby Quilt

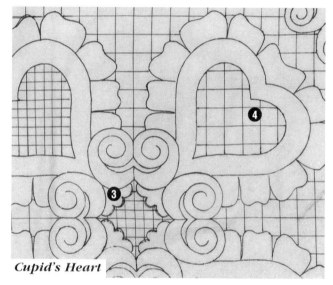

Cupid's Heart

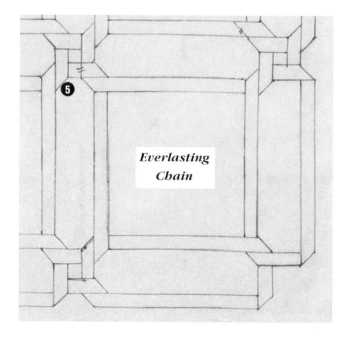

Everlasting Chain

Moroccan
Grid
2½"

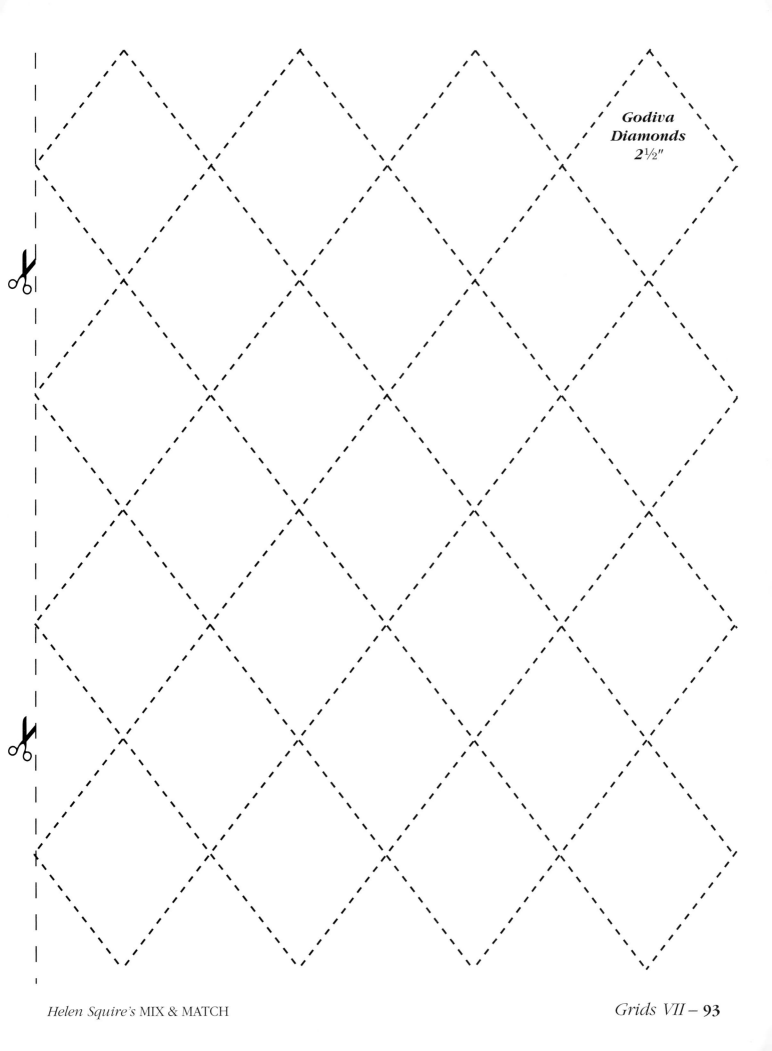

Godiva
Diamonds
$2\frac{1}{2}''$

Clamshells
2"

Floral Lei
Continuous Wreath
7"

Chapter Seven

▶ Secondary Designs

☐ In quiltmaking we often use multiple repeats of the same pattern. By itself, *Floral Lei* is a lovely continuous double-line pattern, yet when four repeats are used (see illustrations on page 97) a secondary design is created by the open area formed at the intersection of the wreaths. Called *negative space*, it becomes an entirely new quilting design.

☐ It's easy to adapt a pattern into a straight line for a border or sashing strip. The real design challenge comes when creating multiple repeats for edge-to-edge quilting, as in *Floral Lei Pantograph*. I like to slightly nestle the motifs, thereby minimizing the open space formed between the rows.

**Floral Lei
Pantograph
2¾"**

Discover two choices with a circular design: to position the main motif at **12**, **3**, **6** and **9** o'clock, or to position it at **2**, **4**, **8**, and **10** o'clock. Choose the placement you like the best. Remember that the pattern set on-point will require – and cover – a larger area.

❏ *Double Blessings* (page 35) is a perfect pattern for a strippy quilt. The design lends itself to multiple repeats that can be enlarged to fit any size. Remember a larger pattern calls for additional quilted details!

❏ When ending the design along the sides, a contour or ripple outline (darkened)looks the best.

❏ The straight edge frames the scrollwork and finishes off the borderless quilt.

- *Glorious Chain* (page 38) has been modified to eliminate the "feathers." It can still be marked using the same purchased stencil.

- Referring to the diagram, flip reverse, miter, and repeat, or, use the stencil to mark one-quarter of a muslin master.

- The diamond shape formed by repeated sets can be quilted with stippling to flatten the background.

- A Taj Mahal feeling (darkened) is created by the undulating flow of the original design – a perfect frame for whitework quilts, any type of medallion, or to showcase appliqué or patchwork patterns.

Dresden Medallion 7"

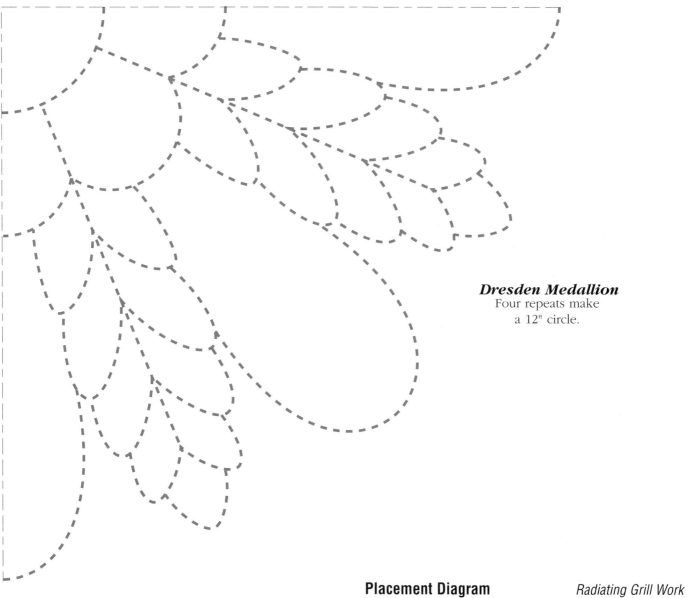

Dresden Medallion
Four repeats make
a 12" circle.

☐ I have a catalog with Indonesian monkeypod wood carvings by Thai artists (see page 53) and handcrafted iron medallion grills by Italian artisans. These techniques, when combined, inspired this international quilting design series.

☐ The pattern reminded me of a 16-petal, appliquéd Dresden Plate arrangement, hence the name *Dresden Medallion*.

☐ Even though it was planned as a quilting pattern, the "petals" could also be appliquéd and a printed leaf fabric substituted for the stylized quilted leaves.

☐ Any circular pattern can be divided into quarters and placed in the corners of a block or project. *Radiating lines* can then be added to extend into the center area.

☐ A gridwork of straight lines is created, flattening the opening between the motifs while enhancing the original rounded design.

Placement Diagram   *Radiating Grill Work*

Rhythmic Geometry
7"

❏ I was both mesmerized and inspired by the undulating movement pulsating throughout the design of a woven Kashmiri wool rug. The *Rhythmic Geometry* quilting pattern series is dedicated to the unknown artisan who created the rug.

❏ When mixing block and border patterns, enlarging sizes might require additional details, while reducing means omitting details and less quilting.

❏ The patterns in this series continue on page 103–105.

- Make four copies of the circle but only one of the center star, to reconnect the entire 12" pattern shown below.

- To create the beautiful secondary design shown on page 105, you need to manipulate the pattern sizes for both *Rhythmic Geometry* and its companion, *Kashmiri Border*, page 104.

- Buy a proportion scale ruler, a handy device sold at quilt shops, wallpaper and art supply stores, or by Golden Threads. To use, line up the measurements of the pattern you have on the *inner* ring and dial what you want on the *outside* ring. The increase or reduction shows in a window opening as a percentage.

Rhythmic Geometry
Four repeats make
a 12" circle.

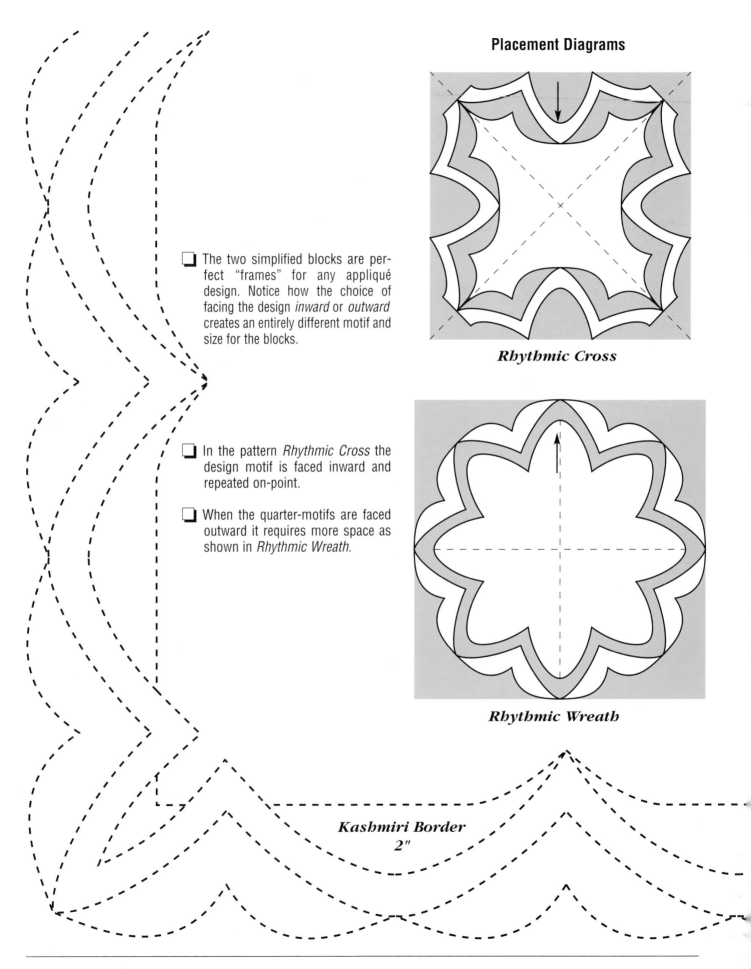

❏ The two simplified blocks are perfect "frames" for any appliqué design. Notice how the choice of facing the design *inward* or *outward* creates an entirely different motif and size for the blocks.

Rhythmic Cross

❏ In the pattern *Rhythmic Cross* the design motif is faced inward and repeated on-point.

❏ When the quarter-motifs are faced outward it requires more space as shown in *Rhythmic Wreath*.

Rhythmic Wreath

Kashmiri Border 2"

Kashmiri Rhythm

☐ The area between the darkened lines of the border and blocks needs background quilting (fillers) added for structure and dimension.

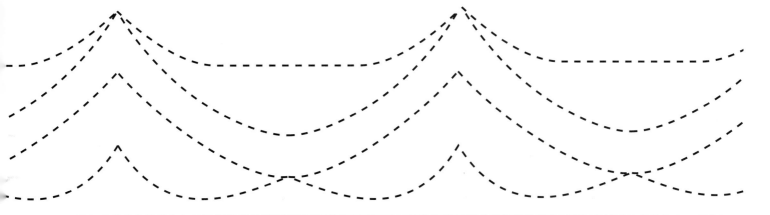

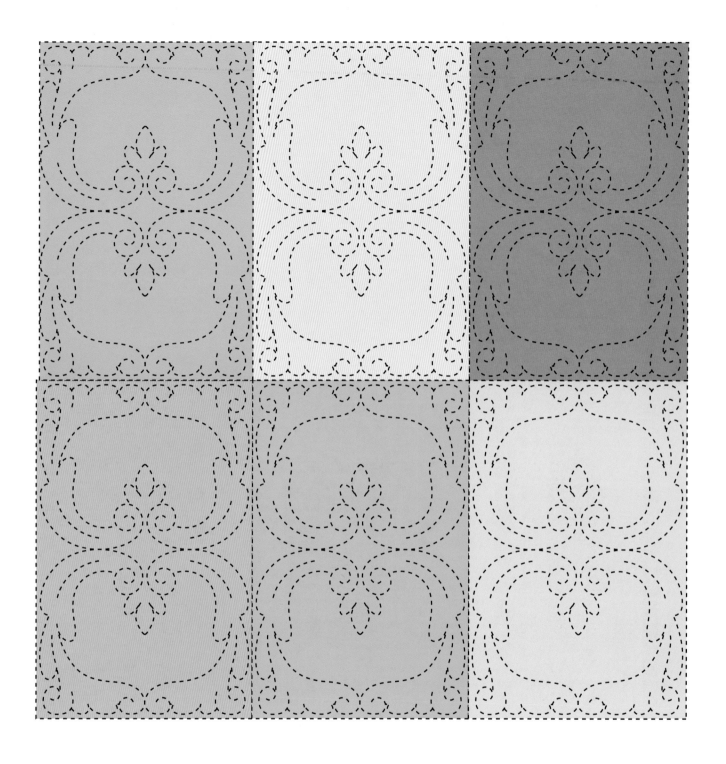

❏ There is a warm visual appeal to this colorful block work quilt. It seems less intimidating than a wholecloth whitework would, even though it takes the same amount of time and talent.

❏ Add quilting in-the-ditch for pieced tops, or draw and quilt straight lines for wholecloths. The lines are needed to balance out the fancy, flowing scrolls of *Whitney* (pages 62–63).

❑ Use multiple copies of *Kaylee* (page 66) to create a strippy quilt. Lock in the fullness along the edges by extending the pattern into the wide binding (see darkened lines). This will prevent the batting from shifting.

**Scalloped Vine
Pantograph – A**
6½"

A

Scalloped Vine Pantograph – B
$6\frac{1}{2}$"

B

Use registration marks to connect sections A and B.

Baby Bunting
3"

110 – *Secondary Designs*

Helen Squire's MIX & MATCH

About the Author

Helen Squire

Providing a masterful mix of patterns that quilters really need, Helen has gained valuable insight by being on both sides of the quilting industry. She combines her quilting experience with entrepreneurial skills to present practical solutions for today's quilter. A graduate of the Fashion Institute of Technology in New York, Helen opened one of the first quilt shops on the East Coast in 1976. Quilt-In, specializing in quilting lessons, supplies, and designs, was followed by Mail-In, which was Helen's mail-order catalog for quilters. As a well-known columnist, Helen has developed a tried and true quilting philosophy through 20 years of writing for Lady's Circle Patchwork Quilts, *in* Dear Helen,...Can You Tell Me?" *and since 1997 for the* American Quilter *magazine in* "Helen's Hints." *She is a recognized authority on quilting patterns and has authored seven books and two CD-ROMs in the* Dear Helen *series. She is technical advisor for the new television series* AMERICAN QUILTER, *as well as vice-president of sales & marketing for American Quilter's Society. Helen resides in Paducah, Kentucky, and invites you to visit her Web site, www.HelenSquire.com.*

Photo credit: Chuck Humbert

◀ **Winterthur Table Runner**

Other AQS Books

This is only a small selection of the books available from the American Quilter's Society. AQS books are known worldwide for timely topics, clear writing, beautiful color photos, and accurate illustrations and patterns. The following books and CDs are available from your local bookseller, quilt shop, or the public library.

#6006 8½"x 11"   US $25.95

#6678 12"x 9"   US $22.95

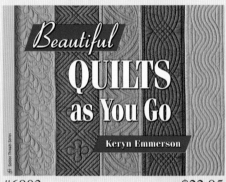

#6803 12"x 9"   US $22.95

& CD-ROMs

#6288   US $29.95

#6099   US $29.95

#5298 17"x 11"   US $16.95

#6571 12"x 9"   US $24.95

#6509 12"x 9"   US $22.95

#6419 12"x 9"   US $24.95

Look for these books nationally. *1-800-626-5420*

Call or *Visit* our Web site at www.AmericanQuilter.com